Anonymous

The Fence Question in the Southern States

Anonymous

The Fence Question in the Southern States

ISBN/EAN: 9783744690294

Printed in Europe, USA, Canada, Australia, Japan

Cover: Foto ©ninafisch / pixelio.de

More available books at **www.hansebooks.com**

THE

FENCE QUESTION

IN

THE SOUTHERN STATES

AS RELATED TO GENERAL

HUSBANDRY AND SHEEP RAISING,

WITH THE HISTORY OF FENCE CUSTOMS, AND LAWS PERTAINING
THERETO: AND A VIEW OF THE NEW FARM SYSTEM
OF THE SOUTH, AS SHOWN IN THE
CENSUS OF 1880.

WASHBURN & MOEN MANUFACTURING CO.

WORCESTER, MASS.

1881.

TABLE OF CONTENTS.

PRESS OF SNOW, WOODMAN & CO., WORCESTER, MASS.

THE FENCE QUESTION IN THE SOUTH.

The United States Department of Agriculture, in its Report for 1871, contained a most elaborate presentment of the statistics of fences in the United States.

These questions had the following range of inquiry 1. Description of fences in use. 2. Height and construction. 3. Estimated rods of fence to each 100 acres of farm lands. 4. Average size of fields. 5, 6, 7, 8. Cost of various kinds of fence. 9. Average cost for repairs. 10. Kinds of wood used. 11. Durability.

In this report, the average cost of fencing, wood being almost exclusively the material in the Southern states, was given as follows

AVERAGE COST PER ROD.

Delaware	1.20	$7,228,274
Maryland	1.25	32,388,370
Virginia	.90	36,742,680
North Carolina	.75	37,392,217
South Carolina	.80	21,136,896
Georgia	.75	45,191,916
Florida	.72	2,459,403
Alabama	.80	36,785,300
Mississippi	.96	25,954,536
Louisiana	1.00	8,182,560
Texas	1.10	33,022,143
Arkansas	.95	18,463,828
Tennessee	.95	62,397,748
West Virginia	.90	32,945,040
Kentucky	.95	76,277,276
Missouri	1.00	64,442,521

The whole cost of the fences in the United States is given in this report at $1,747,549,931 with an annual total outlay for repairs of $93,963,187.

THE HISTORY OF THE FENCE SYSTEM.

The history and meaning of a system whose cost is represented in such solid figures is worth a brief consideration, for there are noteworthy reasons why to-day, as for generations past, the fence holds its place among all people of English descent in all parts of the globe, to a degree found among no other nationalities. These reasons are to be found in the history of the English race, for whom the fence marks the growth of English liberty and the era of new delight in landed possessions. And with these came the earliest spring and growth of a better English husbandry. Neither of these were possible until the military and oppressive attributes of the feudal system in tenures of property gave way before the rising spirit of freedom. These oppressive tenures were already beginning to be a thing of the past, when Sir John Fortescue, about the middle of the fifteenth century, one of the earliest English writers who refers to this subject, declared in his "De laudibus legum Angliæ" (1463).

"The importance of having the land inclosed is generally admitted. Even the feeding lands are likewise surrounded with hedge rows and ditches."

The earliest English writer on rural affairs, Sir A. Fitzherbert, in his "Book of Husbandry" (1532) which it is acknowledged gave the first marked stimulus to English farming, strongly urged the inclosure of land as the very foremost principle of good husbandry. He advises all landlords to grant leases to farmers who will **divide their farms into** proper inclosures ; by which operation, he says.

" *If an acre of land be worth sixpence rental, before it is inclosed, it will be worth eightpence when it is inclosed.*"

The oppressions arising from the old military **tenures were** discontinued during the civil wars in the reign of Charles Ist. **and in the time of the** Commonwealth were entirely abolished in a strong movement of the landed gentlemen of England, by express statute under Charles II, (12. C. **II.** *p.* 26 and from that time English farm and rural life assumed permanent **traits** which extended from the mother country to all her colonies and dependencies.

Up to that time there had existed in all parts of the kingdom, even in the vicinity of the large towns, vast areas of common and waste fields so incumbered by mixed tenures and customs that their cultivation **was** impossible. By special acts of Parliament on petition of commoners interested, one after another these commons were laid out, subdivided and inclosed by special **commissioners.** The first act on the subject of commons, had in the time **of** Henry III, (20 H. III, c. 4) defined the rights of lords of manors to improve to the profits of their tenants, by inclosing, cultivating, or building **upon** the woods, wastes, and common pastures.

The first of the "Inclosure Acts" so called, **upon** whose fruits the pride and beauty of rural England so largely rest, was passed under Charles II ; the next under Queen Anne. At considerable intervals these acts followed, in the face of much opposition, **the movement** becoming general early in the last century. Thus from 1719 **to 1759 there were** 249 acts ; from 1764 to 1777 their number was 941, an average **of 58** annually ; from 1780 to 1794, there were 445. In 1795, and **1796** the number **was 144**, and from 1797 **to** 1805 there were 794. In the **first** forty years **of the** reign of George **III**, there **were** 1213 Inclosure Acts covering 1,960,189 **acres.**

The total area of land inclosed by 2591 **Acts up to the end of 1805 was** 4,187,056 acres. Since then **these** acts have **been very numerous, even in** our own time.

Referring to **this** subject, Blackstone says.(*Commentaries* 3d. *vol.* p. 188.) "The cultivation **of** common lands, and the inclosure and management **of** them are now (1765) carried on under private Acts of Parliament, subject to the regulation laid down in 13 George III, c. 81, and 41 Geo. III c. **109,** which are incorporated into all special inclosure Acts."

"Thus," says a writer on British rural affairs (1816) "the commons, and common fields," a disgrace to English Agriculture, are being wiped away."

The principle and custom of fence prescriptions established in these Inclosure Acts will be understood from the following notes of a case at issue given in *The Jurist* (*Vol.* 9. *N. S.* 60). By the 13th Section of the Act of 50 Geo. **III** for enclosing the lands of the parish of Gosforth the commissioners are required "to allot and set out by marks and bounds so much of the commons and waste grounds as shall seem necessary, and to sell the same ; and the purchasers thereof, their heirs and assigns, shall be liable to make and keep in repair such part of the ring or outer fences **as** shall be directed **by** the commissioners."

NOTES ON ENGLISH FENCING.

That the English fence was designed to be something more than **a** boundary mark, as the old time furrow, trench, or simple barrier, may be understood from an early work on advanced English Agriculture, (*General View of the Agriculture of Devon* 1813,) which gives a view of **the modes of** fencing resorted to. In one instance (*p.* 133) there occurs this **description.**

Raising a mound on a nine feet base, with a ditch three feet wide on each side (making the whole site of the fence fifteen feet) facing the mound four feet high with stones sodded three feet higher above the stone work, and leaving it four and a half feet broad on the top.   Then planting the top with two rows of hawthorne.

This is, safely enough, spoken of by this writer as " a fence that is permanently efficient for the purpose of subdivision and boundary as well as an excellent protection for stock."   The size of these inclosures varied from six to eight and ten acres.

In another case of enclosure on the Black Down Hills in Devon, under Act of Parliament,

"The outside and partition fences of all the new allotments are laid out on a ten feet base, upon which a mound with sodded sides is raised five feet high, and left six feet wide at the top. These banks are all enclosed with a ditch four feet wide and three feet deep.   On each brow of the mound a wattled fence about two feet high, within which is planted the double hedge-row. On the top of the mound, two rows of withy or sallow cuttings, placed three feet apart. Between these are planted oak, ash, beech, birch, alder, hazel, dog-wood, or thorns, and at a distance of every ten feet along the middle of the mound, alternate, Scotch and spruce fir are planted.   The size of these inclosures varies from five to eight acres."

The results of this change in the land system, which has through many generations been adapting the area of England to the home and uses of many tillers of the soil, are in the same direction with the present tendency of land divisions in the Southern States, the effects and possibilities of which we shall discuss further on in these pages.   According to Mr. Caird, (*Landed Interest*), in Great Britain there are about 560,000 tenant farmers, of whom seventy per cent occupy less than fifty acres each ; twelve per cent between fifty and one hundred acres ; eighteen per cent over one hundred acres.   Five thousand occupy between five hundred and one thousand acres each.

How general became this transformation of English commons into close fields, and the effect of the system, is well told in the report of Henry Colman, an eminent American agricultural authority, who made an extended tour in Europe in 1844, and has given in his valuable work the following reference to the inclosures of Great Britain.

"The farm inclosures in England are of various extent, from ten to twenty and fifty acres. In some parts of England they resemble the divisions of New England farms, and are of various sizes, but generally small and of all shapes, often not exceeding four or five acres.   It is reported of a farmer of Devonshire that he lately cultivated over one hundred acres of wheat in fifty different fields.   On a Staffordshire farm a sixty-five acre turnip field was in eight inclosures.   It was subsequently divided into three fields, and nearly half a mile of fence saved.   Ninety-one acres in the same neighborhood were originally in twenty-seven inclosures.   Some of the fences in the latter instance occupied land from three to four yards wide that the plough never touched. In parts of Lincolnshire, inclosures average fifty acres each, and in the fens, or redeemed lands, the ditches are the only fences.   In Northumberland and the Lothians the inclosures are extensive, and, excepting on the out-lines, there are no fences.   In Berkshire, it has latterly become the practice to remove inner fences, and leave the fields open."

It will be of interest to close this reference to English fencing by a view of to day, from an intelligent observer.   Richard Grant White in his recent volume on *Rural England*, says.

"The notion that the hedge is the universal fence in England, is erroneous.   Even in the south, where hedges are most common, post and rail fences are even more common ; for the hedge is used chiefly on the road-line, and to mark the more important divisions of property. Elsewhere, post and rail fences and palings are frequently found.   The hedges that line the roads are generally not more than three feet and a half high, and are not thick, but grow so thin and hungrily that the light shines through them.   Near houses, especially in suburban places, brick walls are common ; and I observed in these a fact which seemed significant.   In most cases I saw that the walls in such places had been raised by an addition of some three feet.   The upper courses of bricks were plainly discernible to be of a make different from that of the original wall, and the joints and the newer mortar could easily be detected.   This seemed to show, unmistakably, an increase in the feeling of reserve, and perhaps in the necessity for it. The walls that would sufficiently exclude the public a hundred years and more ago, were found insufficient, and some fifty years ago (for even the top courses were old, and well set, and mossy) the barriers were made higher,—high enough to be screens against all passing eyes."

In other words, modern England is not departing from the principle of close fencing, and if there be any marked tendency in modern times it is to make the fence and inclosures even more exclusive. An extract from a leading English journal, of a comparatively recent date, has an interest as bearing upon this point, that in England to-day the fence has become a barrier successfully to be maintained, even against the time honored practice of cross-country riding in the fox hunt.

> Hunting men will be a little astonished at the decision of Lord, Coleridge, and Mr. Justice Mellor in the case of Paul and Summerhayes, last Saturday. Till now it has been assumed—wrongfully as it seems—that a field of horsemen following the hounds in full cry, have a right to ride anywhere and everywhere. Damage to growing crops might' perhaps be recovered, but the right to go anywhere, to jump hedge and ditch, to cross ploughed land and meadow, was hardly ever questioned. It is now authoritatively announced that no such right exists. This decision can scarcely fail to have practical results. (*Pall Mall Budget, Nov.* 20th., 1878.)

From this brief review of historical facts pertaining to the fence, it will be seen that it has become an important trait of English character and race history for many generations past.

FIELD SYSTEMS OF OTHER NATIONS.

The care for boundary lines indeed is found in the oldest history, sacred and profane. The law of Moses, interpreted by Josephus, declares that "Whosoever is capable of removing the boundaries of land, is not far from a disposition to violate other laws." Solon's laws of Greece were rigid in the extreme.

> "If any man makes a hedge near his neighbor's ground let him not pass his neighbor's land marks. If he builds a wall, he is to leave one foot between him and his neighbor, if a house two feet. Olive and fig-trees must be planted nine feet from another's ground." (*Aristot. Polit.* 11. 8.

In ancient Greece much of the country was open pasture, for there was no agriculture. In that period small portions of land for choice and more secluded uses, were carefully enclosed, but the tilled fields were open.

Roman law punished offences against boundaries with great severity. Indeed the respect of the ancients for land-marks literally amounted to adoration, for according to Ovid and Juvenal, one Roman ruler commanded oblations to be made to them.

These general features of ancient land systems are found among modern nations, where they still have relation to, or carry the traditions of the state of society and government, and thus both in fact and meaning offer striking contrasts to the fence system that has become one of the most common attributes of English freedom.

In France, Austria, and many parts of Germany, all the arable lands are generally uninclosed, even where agriculture is highly advanced. Fences of hedge or palings may be seen near towns and larger villages for home inclosures, but in general the whole rural country is open, and the boundaries of estates are marked by stones, heaps of earth, or rows of trees. The cattle are either soiled, or tended while at pasture. Under the best developements of this system, guards are established throughout the country to prevent depredations by stray beasts.

This system in French agriculture is much commented on and admired by aesthetic letter writers, but furnishes no example Americans or Englishmen would be willing to see reproduced on their soil. Says Dr. Loring, United States Commissioner of Agriculture, in a recent paper on *Land Holding* :

"It is true that the French farmers are citizens of a Republic, and are owners of the soil on which they live ; but it is a Republic without the traditions of freedom; a soil divided among them by violence before they had reached the point of citizenship. • • • • •
There the home known to the American farmer is not found. The American farm house is almost unknown. The peasantry gather for the night into crowded towns away from their lands and go forth by day to till their few outlying acres. (*Problem of American Landholding, 1881.*")

In less advanced nations, as Russia and Poland, until within a very few years, all cultivated lands have been uninclosed, patches of open pasture and plowed lands appearing here and there in the interminable forest and wilderness tracts. But Herbert Barry an intelligent English traveller in his " Russia in 1870 " finds it among the earliest results of the abolition of Russian serfdom, that " the fields are better fenced."

In Spain the lands are everywhere open, and in Sweden there are but few fences. Italy to day has no more fences than in the days of the Roman Empire, when the avocation of the herdsman gave him his place in classic poetry. Says a writer : " Tityrus and Menalcas would have had something else to do than sit under a wide spreading beech tree, and blow their rustic reeds, if the want of inclosures had not rendered their services indispensable to prevent their flocks from straying."

It will thus be seen that the absence of fences belongs to the earliest times and the rudest husbandry, or to present systems that reflect past oppressions ; and that inclosed fields have a most important relation to the progress of civil liberty, which protects and enhances for the individual proprietor his enjoyment of exclusive possession of soil.

THE FENCE IN AMERICA.

The spirit of the English people, and the early history and meaning of English land enclosures, was already well shaped at the period when offshoots from the home country made the English settlements in America. The Englishman's love of land owning, and pride in his separate possession of the soil, was intensified by the finding fuller scope in the wildernesses of a new continent to be tamed and portioned. There were no old military tenures to narrow and impair such possession, for these had passed away in England.

By the original patents from the crown to the first American colonies, shown in the charters of Maryland, Virginia, Georgia and the Carolinas, as the parents of all tenures in the Southern states, the lands were granted to the patentees not as a feature of political government, in the old feudal meaning, but only as the source of the rules of holding and transmitting real property between man and man. Thus the people of the state became the original source of titles, and all land was made allodial, or free, and fence laws were among the first to appear in the colonial statute books, as they still are among the first in our new territories. (*See laws of Colorado* 1877 : *Oregon* 1854 : *Arizona* 1877 *Idaho* 1878.)

COMMON LAW AND FENCE PRESCRIPTIONS.

Ancient Brehon statutes in Ireland, the foundation of English law, established careful regulations and penalties pertaining to the trespassing and injury done by beasts, but contained no fence prescriptions.

At the common law no man is bound to fence his lands against the cattle of another. An owner of cattle must keep his beasts strictly upon his own land, and he becomes a trespasser if they go upon the land of another, whether such land is fenced or not. In other words, at common law the owner of animals must fence them in—his neighbor is not bound to fence them out. It was necessary therefore, at common law that every man should maintain a personal watch over his own animals, or surround his land with a fence.

Important modifications of the common law were made necessary by the situation in which the English colonists found themselves in this country at first arrival, and for a long time afterward. For want of proper pasturage, and from the vast extent of unimproved lands, it was necessary and desirable that the cattle should be permitted to go at large for subsistence, and in the sparse settlements and scarcity of inhabitants it was impossible to watch the beasts to prevent their trespass upon improved lands. Every land owner therefore was required by statutory provisions to erect and maintain sufficient fences about his cultivated tracts, or forego all compensation for damages from trespassing beasts, in the absence or insufficiency of such fences. In every state in the union, from the earliest times, it has been made compulsory the land owner to maintain good fences for the protection of crops; to to fence the animals *out*, rather than to fence them *in*.

It has been abundantly established as perfectly competent for the legislatures of the several states to pass laws regulating the subject of boundary and division fences; and that inasmuch as the common law does not require parties to maintain fences, statutes regulating the same are remedial, and intended to adapt existing defects in the common law to the special needs or customs of communities.

But all such modifications are made the subject of express statutes. Indeed the sole obligation to fence is founded upon some agreement, or statute prescription. Thus the rule for partition fences adapts itself to the condition of two adjoining land owners, upon each of whom rests the care of his own beasts. Each must fence against the other, if he cares to fence at all; and as two parallel fences would be useless expense, the provision exists requiring and enforcing maintenance by each, of his own portion of the dividing fence. It is a well established principle of fence law that no one but the adjoining owners or possessors have any interest in the duty or obligation to build or maintain a division fence, which exists only as against the adjoining tracts, where both owners seek benefits from the fence.

Another important modification of the common law, now reappearing in new legislation in several Southern states, pertains to ring or circular fences, built and maintained by owners of tracts enclosed for common protection of their fields; thus kept within such enclosures without the expense of inner partition fences. This custom, in some form, has prevailed in America from the earliest settlement.

SOUTHERN FENCE LAWS.

The southern fence system has from the first been strongly marked with these general facts of fence history, and the particular discriminations referred to, derived from special local needs and customs.

By the laws of most of the Southern states the owner of stock is under no obligation to restrain them to his own grounds, and is not responsible for their trespasses on the lands of others not properly fenced (7 *Jones* 468), and this principle is not changed by the new system of fencing to inclose large tracts, by counties or townships. As to strictness of the rule of "sufficient fences" it has been held by a common court in a case of trespass, that if any part of the enclosure trespassed upon be under a fence of less than the prescribed height, though it was shown that the beasts had passed at a part of the fence of lawful height, the plaintiff could not recover, the court declaring that the law will presume the cattle were first tempted to break into the enclosure by reason of the lowness of other parts of the fence. (*Cowen* 421.)

At a very early day in South Carolina a plaintiff plead the local custom of the place and recovered half the cost of a partition fence, on appeal the court above holding the custom a good one. (2 *Brevard* 67). The Supreme Court of Alabama a few years since declared that the legal obligation of tenants of adjoining lands to make and maintain partition fences depends entirely upon statutory provisions. (24 *Ala.* 310). A Maryland decision of the highest court holds that where no act of the legislature exists, the principles of common law prevail, and unless by force of prescription one need not fence against an adjoining close, but he is bound at his peril to keep his cattle on his own land. (11 *Md.* 340.)

Nor have these prescriptions as to the legal and sufficient fence been displaced by the stringent ordinances that in many of the states forbid cattle going at large. In states where stray animals have been for years prohibited under severe penalties, such obligation to fence remains unchanged. So far from becoming obsolete, amendments to existing fence laws and systems are numerous and recent in many of the states, and, as before shown, a stringent fence law is sure to be among the first to be placed upon the statute books of new states and territories. Indeed, there is no part of the United States where a good and sufficient fence is not either specifically enjoined, or it is made the land owner's interest, if he be also a planter, to build one.

"THE LEGAL FENCE" IN THE SOUTH.

According to U. S. Report for 1871, more than one-half of the farm area is woodland. Worm fence is almost the exclusive mode, the proportion being 96 per cent. Garden and homestead fences are generally of palings. In returns from 37 counties in North Carolina there is only a single record of post and rail fence. Five feet is the legal height fixed for fences in most, if not all the cotton States. Chestnut, oak and pine are the woods most used. In Mississippi half the counties report that no other fence but worm is in use. In some of the Louisiana parishes where hedges had been in extensive use, these have largely died out from the effects of frost and neglect, and injury during the war. About two-thirds of the inclosures of Louisiana are surrounded with the Virginia fence.

Worm fence constitutes three-fourths of the fencing in Texas. Live fence is used in many portions of the state. Ditches 5 feet deep, 6 feet wide at the top, and three feet at the bottom, the earth thrown up on the side of the field enclosed, are made in sections where timber is not easy to be produced.

In Virginia and Maryland a lawful fence is thus described :

" A lawful fence must be 4 feet high if made of stone, and 5 feet high if made with any other material, and so close that the beast breaking into the same could not creep through; or with a hedge 2 feet high upon a ditch 3 feet deep and 3 feet broad; or, instead of such a hedge, a rail fence, of 2 1-2 feet high, the hedge or fence being so close that none of the creatures aforesaid can creep through."

The height and character of the legal fence in the Southern States vary but slightly, though a wide selection of material is allowed. Throughout the South, adhering more strictly to English models of emphatic fencing, the prescriptions have universally called for a fence from six to twelve inches higher than is required in other parts of the United States ; FIVE FEET being the almost universal height of the legal fence in the South.

Indeed by very many who are interested in the relation of the fence question to the developement of southern farming, it is held to be injurious and oppressive that the fence required under the law, and by custom, needs not only a greater height than in other states, but far greater closeness at the bottom than is usual in any other parts of this country. Pig-tight fences are very expensive, and yet in many districts the pig dominates in fence considerations to an extent widely beginning to be complained of. Many farmers and

planters are beginning to believe that the **swine at least** should be relegated to the rule of the common law.

In Maryland, indeed, there is no general fence law, **but fence** and herd regulations are left to be made for the several counties by special laws. In Louisiana, though fence practice is not greatly different from other Southern States, no legal fence is prescribed, the fence system having **been originally** shaped **on** French modes in the early settlement. With such modifications the fence laws of the Southern States have always been stringent and specific, **and** for reasons before indicated, it has generally been held incumbent on **the** planter and field owner to adequately protect his crops, if he would have legal remedy against trespassing beasts.

THE SOUTHERN HERD LAWS.

This general view of **the** Southern fence system is made complete by a brief review of the herd and cattle laws of the Southern states, drawn from some of their oldest statutes that have never become obsolete.

In Delaware, cattle are forbidden to run at large in certain districts.

In Maryland, damages sustained by trespassing animals are recovered by sale of animals.

Virginia **statutes make** the owner **responsible for the** damages from trespassing animals, in any ground enclosed **by a lawful fence;** for each succeeding trespass by the same animals, double **damages; after two** previous trespasses, in five days notice, the animals to be **forfeited to the** aggrieved party.

In North Carolina, damages for injury by trespassing animals **are** recoverable against the owner, and by distraint of the animals.

In South Carolina, animals breaking into a field **enclosed with a lawful fence** are held for such damages; but full satisfaction lies **for injuring any animal** found in any field where the fence is defective.

In Georgia the fields must be protected by a lawful fence, or **damages for** trespass will not lie against **the** owner of the animal, and if the **trespassing** animal be killed or injured **by** the owner **of the** field, treble damages **may be** collected.

In Florida there can be **no** trespass if the fence is not a lawful **one.**

In Alabama any animal running at large may be taken up, **and charges** collected before a justice of the peace.

In Mississippi a ranger is elected in each county to attend to estrays. Owners of animals are responsible for all damages in grounds enclosed by a legal fence. Stray animals must be delivered to the ranger.

Texas laws forbid all **neat** cattle belonging **to** non-residents being taken into **the** State for grazing or herding purposes.

In Arkansas if the fence be legal, the owner **of the** trespassing animals is liable for all damages; **for** the second offence **in double** damages, and for the third trespass by the same animals, the **party injured** may kill the animals without being answerable.

In Tennessee the laws of estrays **are limited** to certain animals.

There is no law in force in West **Virginia to** prevent cattle running at large, **but where the** fence is lawful the **owner of the** animals is liable for all **damages** from trespass.

In Kentucky the **owner** must protect his fields with a legal fence. The law of estrays applies only to male animals and distempered cattle.

Missouri herd laws have been made **very** strict by alarm as to diseases from Texas and Mexican cattle. The rights **of** the owner of **a field** enclosed by a legal fence are the same as in other States.

Still another relation of fencing to **southern communities** deserves a brief **reference.** According to Poor's Manual for 1881, **there** were 93,671 miles of

railroad in operation in the United States at the close of the year 1880 ; of
this number 24,120 miles are divided among the Southern States as follows :

Miles of Railroad in Southern States in 1880.

STATES.	MILES.
Maryland	1012
Virginia	1826
North Carolina	1499
South Carolina	1429
Georgia	2535
Florida	530
Alabama	1851
Mississippi	1183
Louisiana	633
Texas	3293
Arkansas	896
Missouri	4011
Tennessee	1824
Kentucky	1598
Total	24,120

In every Northern and Western state railroad companies are required either
by the express terms of their charters, or by general statutes to maintain
" good and sufficient fences " along their tracks, and the later tendency has
been to make these laws more explicit and imperative.

SOUTHERN RAILROADS AND FENCING.

But in the Southern states the specific rules and customs of railroad fencing
have always been far from strict, and only by indirection, compulsory.

Missouri indeed is to be excepted, her statutes requiring all railroad companies to fence all portions of their lines that run through cultivated land, or
be liable for double the amount of damages done to live stock by the passing
of their trains. In no other Southern state does such a law exist, though
there have been attempts to accomplish the same end ; either as in Kentucky
and Texas by special exemptions from the acts providing damages for injuries
to persons and property, in the cases of railroad companies " whose entire
lines are enclosed with good and lawful fences, and good and sufficient cattle
gaps, kept in good repair,— or by statutes intended to be penal in their
character, as in Tennessee, North Carolina, South Carolina, Alabama, Florida
and Arkansas, whereby railroad companies are held liable in damages, or
double damages for all injuries done to live stock by their trains.

It will be noticed that these constructions and prescriptions of the laws of
the Southern states, applicable to railway fencing, refer chiefly to compensa-
tions for damages to live stock, leaving the security of passengers without
expressed recognition. A marked change has, however, taken place within
the past few years in the Southern railway system, by the absorption and
development of many former small and merely local lines into the great routes
of trans-Continental transit and traffic, and this must bring a better law and
custom in railway fencing making the prime consideration, THE SAFETY OF THE
TRAVELLING PUBLIC.

No better statement has ever been made of the principle of railway fencing
than was given forty-two years ago, at the very commencement of the railroad
era, in an English Parliamentary report, as follows. It is worthy the attention of all Southern legislators.

The good fencing of railroads is essential to the safety of passengers ; and it must
be observed that the bank on which a railway is formed, especially attracts the cattle
by reason of its dryness compared with the adjoining fields, while one small defect in
the fence may endanger the lives of the whole train of passengers.   *   *   *
The power of obliging a railway to make good fences should not be left to the proprietors or occupiers of the adjoining lands who may not be constantly vigilant, or who
may not choose to interfere. (*English Parliamentary Report*, 1839.)

From this brief review it will be seen that, after generations of test and
experience, there has been nothing in the open field husbandry of other nations

that has invited imitation by English speaking people; among whom the "no fence theory" has made little progress. Advocates of this "no fence" theory refer to the common law, of which we have already spoken, and insist that we should return to it. But England is the home of the common law. It is the pride and boast of her people. With all the protection which it is flippantly claimed, the common law gives to open fields, the people of England have more thoughtfully and effectually fenced their grain fields, their pasture fields, their orchard paths, gardens and towns, than any other people in the world; and the fence derived from English custom and practice in the past three hundred years, and in no degree diminished to-day, marks and measures the love of home that characterizes the English born, and the countries to which they have carried English traits.

FENCE BURDENS.

The burdens brought by the system of fencing were presented in the figures given at the outset of this discussion, and are well summed up by the secretary of the Iowa State Agricultural Society in the following statement.

It is declared, even in states where timber of the best quality is abundant, so much so that it is an object to get it off the land, that the cost of fencing their lands *exceeds the cost of the buildings for the comfort of the inhabitants.* How much greater must be the cost of fences in states where most of the land is entirely destitute of timber. (*Iowa State Ag. Report* 1863.)

For many years past the question has been a pressing one, what shall we do for fences; and what better economy can be found for their construction. The fence of rails, pole, or brush, however cheap the material, represents a large outlay for labor in erection and repairs; to be effective it must be cumbersome; it occupies and holds out of use a large amount of arable land. It is subject to rapid decay. It is easily destroyed by fire. Its material is easily stolen and carried off. It is easily thrown down or broken down. Floods carry it off. In regions of quick growths it is a jungle of weeds. The fence most widely in use in the South is the worm fence, the rails laid with their ends resting on each other, occupying and rendering useless a strip four feet in width on each side. "Every mile of such fence occupies and wastes nearly two acres of ground. The loss by such fences in the State of New York is estimated at three hundred thousand acres of good farming land. (*Register Rural Affairs,* 1860.) In English fencing, as may well be believed from what we have before written, the loss in land area from old systems of fencing is even greater than this. An eminent English Agriculturist estimates that hedges in many districts in England occupy *one-fifth of the soil.*

For many reasons the attempt for the universal adoption of the hedge in American fencing, very actively made many years ago, most entirely failed. The hedge is practically out of discussion by our American planters and farmers, for reasons urged long ago for their eradication in England, lovely as are the hedgerows of England in memory and in song. We quote from a standard source, this English indictment against the hedge. It is equally applicable to this country

"1. Hedge fences are injurious, and that to a great extent, because they harbor and are a protection to all sorts of weeds.
"2. They harbor and protect snails and slugs and other enemies of the crop.
"3. They harbor a great many birds, and afford them every encouragement in building nests.
"4. They are highly objectionable on account of their size.
"5. They are injurious because they drain and impoverish the soil in their vicinity, amounting to a serious loss to the farm area of England, when the number and extent of the hedges is considered." (*Journal English Agricultural Society* 1844.)

If common lumber be the resort for fence material as it has largely been, the forests are rapidly wasting away, and it is becoming each year more costly.

For a century and a half a large population has been consuming and wasting the best timbered region on the continent—that lying between the Atlantic and the Mississippi River—and the consumption of lumber for building, fencing, implements, railroads. etc., is increasing with gigantic strides.

The fence question **has been** taken up and discussed with great intelligence by State Boards **of Agriculture**, notably that of Kentucky, the Report **of** which latter Board. in 1878, contains the following :

There are in Kentucky 125,000 farms, which will average 600 rods of fencing to the farm. This will aggregate 75,000,000 rods, chiefly of the old " worm fence," which still holds its preponderance. To build this amount of fencing will call for 2,000,000,000 rails, and not less than 70,-000,000 rail trees. To keep this amount of fencing in repair will call for a yearly consumption of 280,000,000 rails and the destruction of ten millions of timber trees. The money cost for the whole of our fencing, at $1.00 per rod cannot be less than $75,000,000, and the annual cost for repairs and renewals not less than $10,000,000. The census reports make the value of Kentucky farms $311,238,916. The value of the fences—$75,000,000—is therefore nearly one-fourth the total value of the farms. Farmers must learn that fences are costly, and be ready for some plan to help diminish their great cost.

Such facts as these have been widely received as pressing suggestions for fence reform, a better economy in kind and use of material, and in legislation modifying the system of fencing.

THE " NO FENCE " LAWS, SO CALLED.

A movement to do away **with** fences on the boundary line of farms and for the protection of fields, began **in** the legislation of Virginia in 1856, in the passage of a special act for abolishing the general fence law within the limits of King William **County**. In 1857 a special act of a similar nature was made applicable to **a part** of Prince George County. In 1866 the whole principle was embodied **in** an amendment to the general fence law of the State of Virginia, to be adopted at their option by vote in all counties or townships in the state, and in the act of 1873 the county Boards of Supervisors were authorized to adopt the law of 1856 for their own counties. By this Virginia system, since copied in the statutes of North Carolina (1872) Georgia (1872), South Carolina (*extra session* 1877), the parties seeking the benefits of the new system, whether as residents of a county, township or parts of either, are required to build and maintain a " lawful fence " the definition of which remains unchanged in the statutes, on the **outer** boundary of all **such** territory ; as the following from the Virginia **act will** sufficiently show.

Sec. 15. Provides that the boundaries of all counties adopting the fence law of 1866 shall be declared lawful fences. Good and substantial gates to be erected in such enclosing fences at all crossings of public roads—with gate keepers, where the court of the county shall require the same * * * the cost of such outer fences to be equitably distributed among all owners and occupants admitted to the privileges of this act.
Sec. 16. (No domestic animal within such boundaries **to be allowed** to run at large beyond limits of owner's land.)
(Sec. 17-18. Owner of animals liable in double damages **for injury** sustained by such trespassing animals), (*Virginia Rev. Stat.* 1873, p. 795.)

Obviously **this** is not *doing away with fences*, and is improperly termed the " *No-Fence Law*," since it is a modification which seeks a better economy in fences ; for not only must the large territory within named limits be strictly enclosed to keep trespassing animals out, but all animals within such bounds must be carefully kept within the fence enclosures of their owners, since within such defended limits the rule of common law prevails. It is only a new vindication of the utility of the fence, and as we have before shown, this resort itself is nothing new. Circular fences and enclosures in common have had their place in fence customs since the earliest settlements of this country, and are still provided for in many states, in the statutes concerning "common fields."

THE FENCE REMEDY.

We come now to a part of the discussion which we desire to present as little as possible in the language of the manufacturer anxious only to press upon the consumer his article of production. The question has certainly to do with public facts and public benefits, and touches something wider than the interest of the wire maker, when we come to present the reasons why within the past twenty-five years a new fence material, iron and steel wire, has received such general substitution for all other fencing material. Already over FOUR HUNDRED AND FIFTY THOUSAND MILES of wire fencing have been used in the United States, and, in the more modern form of Barb Fencing, it is to-day being supplied at the rate of from 80,000 to 100,000 miles of finished fence annually.

Wire was first commended for fencing purposes sixty years ago, though at that time it was a comparatively scarce and costly article, drawn by hand, the workman's daily stint being from fifteen to forty pounds a day, in place of the present daily yield to each workman of from 1,800 to 2,500 pounds.

In 1816 the Memoirs of the Philadelphia Agricultural Society contain a paper read January 8th, in which instances are given of Wire Fencing already in use, which had demonstrated a great saving of cost to the farmer, in the following estimates:

"Cost of a common fence for 100 acres for fifty years, $3,080; cost of a Wire Fence for the same period, $1,751; leaving a profit of $1,329" the same writer adds: "With regard to the strength of a Wire Fence, we do not hesitate to express our belief in its sufficiency to resist any attack that may be required. We have given it a fair trial at the Falls of Schuylkill (Pa.), with the most breachy cows of the neighborhood, and it is remarkable that even dogs avoid passing over it." For greater protection, the wire was coated with a preparation of linseed oil. The whole article is re-published with illustrations in the *Plough, Loom and Anvil,* for September, 1849.

In 1821 the *American Farmer,* of Baltimore, complaining of the cost and wastefulness of existing fences, urged wire as an "economical and effective resort."

In 1845 the transactions of the New York State Agricultural Society declare wire fencing successful, and urge its "growing necessity." In the same volume, Edward Clark, in the reports of the New York State Agricultural Society for 1845, describes wire fencing and praises its efficiency. He says he "saw it check a furious Bull." He declares that for protection it should be galvanized. The same authority declares hedges "under growing disfavor, as they shelter field-mice, and the enemies of the crops."

In 1847 the New York State Agricultural Society awarded a silver medal for wire fence, as "cheaper and more effective for farm use than wood."

In 1849 among the transactions of the same Society, a wire fence brought out in Niagara County was highly commended as "secure against all animals; a great saving of land; giving no shelter for briars and nettles; proof against high winds; makes no snow drifts; DURABLE AND CHEAPEST AMONG MATERIALS."

In 1849 *The Plough, Loom and Anvil,* of Philadelphia, sharing in the discussion of the period, uttered this wise and far-seeing opinion, that "setting aside merits, the demand for wood fences would *increase the price, while the demand for wire fence will diminish the price,* as the greater the demand for wire the cheaper it can be made." This was speedily realized, and has remained

true in the history of wire manufacture. It is estimated that three hundred and
fifty thousand miles of plain galvanized iron wire was used for fencing purposes
in the twenty years preceding 1870. It was cheap, easily transported, easily
erected, and gave relief and a handy resort for the farmer, especially in the
new fast growing regions of the West and Southwest, where timber was
scarce. But the farmers and herders were never thoroughly happy in its use.
The fence of plain and single wire was susceptible to all changes of temperature. It snapped in cold, and sagged in heat. It had no terrors for cattle.
They pressed up to the boundaries of the pasture, and easily lunched through
the fence on the adjacent crop. Growing more resolute they broke bounds
altogether, or contentedly sawed their itching necks and polls on the smooth
wire, in the acme of creature satisfaction, until the fence gave way. It shows
the stress of fence necessities most strongly, that with all these attendant
evils, the plain wire fence held its place, and grew in use and favor.

BARB FENCING DISCOVERED.

In the year 1873 a practical man in Illinois patented the first defensive
armor for wire fence. This consisted of strips of wood carrying at short
intervals sharpened points of wire. This strip he attached to the old-fashioned,
plain wire fence. The device was taken up with avidity, and widely used in
the Northwest. This barbed strip suspended upon the upper wire of an old-
fashioned plain wire fence, transformed it instantly into a barrier to be re-
spected by the most venturesome animal.

A little later an Illinois citizen realized the Glidden Barb
Fence, far better than the first rude barb contrivance, by
attaching the barbs directly to the fence wires. It was
the achievement of a practical farmer who knew what he
himself needed. His first constructed line of Barb Fence
is still in use in DeKalb County, Illinois, and from this
small beginning dates the era of Barb Fencing. Here is
the short business history of Barb Fencing since that time.

THE GLIDDEN BARB.

Estimated Production of Barb Fencing since 1874.

During the year 1874 there were 10,000 lbs. made and sold.
During the year 1875 there were 600,000 lbs. made and sold.
During the year 1876 there were 2,840,000 lbs. made and sold.
During the year 1877 there were 12,863,000 lbs. made and sold.
During the year 1878 there were 26,655,000 lbs. made and sold.
During the year 1879 there were 50,337,000 lbs. made and sold.
During the year 1880 there were 80,500,000 lbs. made and sold.
During the year 1881 the estimate is for 120,000,000 lbs.

A ton of Barb Wire will make two miles of staunch and perfect three
strand fence. As used by many farmers in lighter construction it will give
proportionately greater length. Barb Wire has become a staple article of
trade. It was at first opposed somewhat bitterly on the score of its professed
and open purpose to *appeal to the sense of pain in the infringing animal.* It
was denounced as cruel, and, more than once, formal resorts have been made
to the State Legislatures for laws to prohibit or restrict its use. In every
such instance the testimony of farmers who have Barb Fence in use, has brought
out and established, even more strongly than before such public inquiry, the
fact that accidents from Barb Fencing are far less numerous, and less serious
than the casualties resulting from the old style of fences. The animal is
instantly repelled by the sharp prick of the Barb, and the most breachy and

venturesome beast soon comes to respect and keep away from the fence. He is not tempted to leaping to his own harm, as by the insecure wooden fence. All classes of animals learn to be orderly and quiet in the enclosures. and let the fence alone.

WHY HAS STEEL BARB FENCE BEEN A SUCCESS?

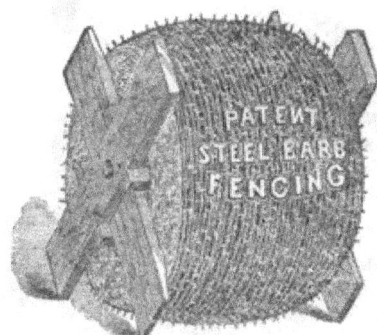

BARB FENCE SPOOL.

FIRST. IT IS STRONG. A strand of Glidden Barb Wire has 2,300 lbs. tensile strength.

SECOND. By the use of a double twisted wire the fence material is strengthened, and at the same time given *the property of adapting itself perfectly to all changes of temperature.* The fence is strong and tight in all seasons.

THIRD. It is the *easiest handled and transported* of fence materials. The usual market package, a compactly wound spool of wire (two of which occupy as freight about the same space as a barrel of flour), weighs 200 pounds and carries 1,400 feet, or over eighty rods of wire. Thus the farmer's team can carry in one load, to any part of his farm, enough fence material to enclose a very large field. The railroad company can transport in a single car-load, Barb Fencing for twenty miles of fence.

The following table will furnish a valuable and perfect means of comparison of Barb Fencing with all other Fence material, as regards weight, and ease of handling.

Table OF WEIGHTS, Showing number of pounds of Barb Fencing required to fence space or distances mentioned, with one, two or three strands.

	1 Strand.	2 Strands.	3 Strands.
1 Foot in length,	1 1-10 oz.	2 1-5 oz.	3 3-10 oz.
100 Feet in length,	7 lbs.	14 lbs.	21 lbs.
1 Rod in length,	1 1-8 lb.	2 1-4 lbs.	3 3-8 lbs.
100 Rods in length,	113 lbs.	226 lbs.	339 lbs.
1 Mile in length,	365 lbs.	730 lbs.	1095 "
1 Square Mile,	1460 "	2920 "	4380 "
1 Square Acre,	58 "	116 "	174 "
1 Square Half Acre,	41 "	82 "	123 "

FOURTH. It is EASILY ERECTED. And this furnishes the reason for the rapid introduction of Barb Fence Material, among all classes of land owners, small farmers and large, and especially among railroad companies with whom the transportation of timber for fencing, to points of use along their railroad lines, is a serious question involving much expense and labor. We have already referred to the ease of handling Barb Fence Wire. A few words as to its ease of erection into a substantial and suitable fence. And this varies with the views and uses of the farmer, for there is no end to the combinations that can be formed with Barb Fencing and other styles of fence. Thus one

line or strand strung on any wooden fence, makes a structure
cattle will not molest. One or two barbed lines or strands put up
with the old plain wire, makes a magical change in the efficiency of
the whole.

The number of strands of Barb Fencing to be used must be deci-
ded in each case by the special object to be accomplished by the
fence.

THE DAVIS STRETCHER.

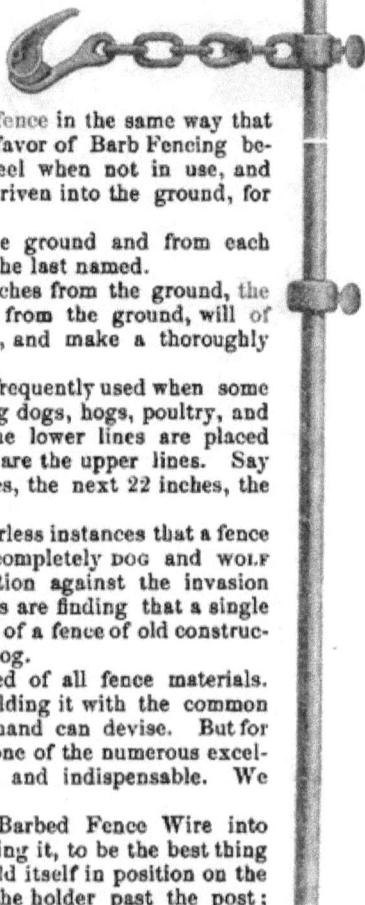

One line of fencing, 3½ feet from the
ground, will turn cows, oxen and horses,
andprotect growing and the most tempt-
ing crops from the larger domestic animals. In many instances the fencing
is kept on a reel and used as a transient fence in the same way that
hurdles are employed ; the advantage in favor of Barb Fencing being that it is compactly wound on the reel when not in use, and
may be readily attached to light stakes, driven into the ground, for
cattle never press against it.

Two lines of fencing, 21 inches from the ground and from each
other, will turn small cattle, as well as the last named.

Three lines of fencing, the lowest 12 inches from the ground, the
next 24 inches, and the third 42 inches from the ground, will of
course better accomplish all named above, and make a thoroughly
good and substantial farm fence.

Four and five strands of fencing are frequently used when some
special object is in view, such as excluding dogs, hogs, poultry, and
other small animals ; in which cases the lower lines are placed
nearer the ground and to each other than are the upper lines. Say
the lowest line 5 inches, the next 12 inches, the next 22 inches, the
next 48 inches from the ground.

It has been tested and proved in numberless instances that a fence
for the protection of sheep may be built completely DOG and WOLF
PROOF. It may be made a perfect protection against the invasion
of swine. For the latter use, many farmers are finding that a single
line of Barb Wire stretched at the bottom of a fence of old construction, will protect their fields against the hog.

Barb Fencing is the most easily treated of all fence materials.
Many small buyers find no trouble in building it with the common
hauling tackle or levers any clever farm hand can devise. But for
fence building on any larger scale, some one of the numerous excellent Stretchers will be found economical and indispensable. We
illustrate two of these :

The Warren Stretcher, for stretching Barbed Fence Wire into
position on the posts, is said, by those using it, to be the best thing
yet invented for that purpose. It will hold itself in position on the
post while the wire is being made fast in the holder past the post ;
giving an opportunity to make the wire fast on the end post, thus
keeping all the strain until the wire is made secure. One man can use it to
very good advantage. It is made of malleable iron, and is light and strong.

The Davis Stretcher is a tool which every one building Barb Fencing
will prize ; it is made very strong. The lever, or bar, is of steel, and is made
to fit the reel, by using the collar (see cut) ; thus the reel can be kept in place
while unreeling the wire. This is very important, as it allows the wire to un-
reel evenly, and makes it much easier for those doing the work. This Stretcher
answers a double purpose, for the same parties unreeling the fencing can
stretch and fasten it into place. It can be used on a large tree, as well as on a
post. Its bearing on the posts does not cause the post to turn in the ground.

These marked features, constituting special adaptedness to Southern needs of fencing, are more fully to be discussed on succeeding pages, but it may be said here that whether for the large land owner, with whom a large percentage of saving in a great outlay for fencing large tracts, is a prime consideration; or whether for the small farmer or tenant who must needs fence economically or go without fencing, Barb Wire meets all requisitions as no other fence material can do. The few acres or the small garden can, at very little expense, be made proof against all trespassers, man or beast, and where desired, it can be put up by the purchaser without any other tools and appliances than the humblest home can easily supply.

FIFTH. It is IMPERISHABLE. Within the past few years, since the introduction of the Bessemer process, steel has largely taken the place of iron in wire for common uses. Steel Barb Wire Fencing is strong, and makes a staunch fence. It is protected from

THE WARREN STRETCHER.

the action of the elements by galvanizing. Thus constructed, it cannot be destroyed by Fire, Wind or Flood, all of these widely recognized as destructive agencies, dreaded by land owners and railroad companies. The sweeping fire leaves the Barb Fence unharmed, for in many instances the fire in light grass or rubbish does not burn long enough to destroy the posts, and the Barb Fence has no other material to feed it. In many cases where the wood fence is strong enough to withstand cattle, it offers a bulk to winds that prostrate it. This has been a serious trouble in open regions. Barb Fencing presents nothing to be affected by the most furious gale. There are numerous locations in bottom lands where the farmer must forego a fence, or replace it every season after the flood and freshet have done their work. Hundreds of miles of Barb Fencing have been built in bottom lands, that have stood unimpaired by overflows.

SIXTH. IT IS THE CHEAPEST EFFICIENT FENCE IN USE. We commenced this discussion with the official statement of the average cost of fencing in the Southern States. In some of them, especially in the Southwest where timber is scarce, it is absolutely impossible for the farmer to fence well, and meet the heavy cost of transporting lumber from a distance. And when the fence of lumber is erected and in place, it is as has already been stated, a serious consideration, how often the fence, or large portions of it, may require renewal in destruction by fire or prostrating winds. These are all parts of the question of the cost of fencing. But we are here to make a fair comparison of the original cost of various kinds of fencing. We have only brought into the comparison Barb Fences of three or four strands, of the staunchest construction. Thousands of miles of Barb Fencing are in use in all parts of the United States, where a single strand of Barb Wire is fastened directly upon trees, at a cost of a little more than twelve cents a rod, yet serving as an effective fence for the pastures of large animals.

COMPARATIVE COST OF FORTY RODS **OF DIFFERENT** KINDS OF FENCE.

THREE BOARD.

1000 feet Pine Fencing, at $15 per M. . $15 00	
80 Posts, at 20 cents each............	16 00
15 lbs. Nails, at 4 cents per lb... . .	60
Labor	2 50

$34 10
Or 85 cents per rod.

THREE GLIDDEN STEEL BARBED WIRE.
14 1-2 feet to the pound.

136 lbs. Japanned or Painted Barb	
.Fencing, at 10 cents $13 60	
40 Posts, at 20 cents each 8 00	
2 lb. Staples (Galvanized), at 10 cents.	20
Labor..................	...50

$22 30
Or 56 cents per rod.
Galvanized Fencing, 59 cents per rod.

FOUR BOARD.

1350 feet Pine Fencing, **at $15** per M...$20 25	
80 posts at 20 cents **each.. .. . .**	16 00
20 lbs. Nails, at 4 cents **per lb**...... .	80
Labor	3 00

$40 05
Or $1.00 per **rod.**

FOUR GLIDDEN STEEL BARBED WIRE.

182 lbs. Japanned or Painted Steel Barb	
Fencing, at 10 cents...............	18 20
40 Posts, at 20 cents **each.. .**	8 00
3 lbs. Staples, at 10 **cents**......... ...	30
Labor........	75

$27 25
Or 68 cents per rod.
Galvanized, **73** cents per rod.

WEIGHT OF GLIDDEN STEEL BARB FENCING.—14 1-2 feet to the **pound.** 7 pounds to 100 **feet.** 365 pounds to one mile.

The following **is the** cost of various styles of Fence, **including** posts :

Narrow Slat Picket Fence ....$6 00 per rod		Glidden Steel **Barb Fence,** four	
Wide '' '' '' .... 5 25 ''		wires ....$ .68 per rod.	
Common Stone Wall.............. 2 25 ''		Glidden Steel Barb Fence, three	
'' Four Board Fence....... 1 00 ''		wires. .... .56 ''	
'' Split Rail Fence.. .... 75 ''		Glidden Steel Barb Fence, two	
		wires......................... .. .36 ''	

SEVENTH.   It is self DEFENSIVE.   It borrows from nature's own barrier, **the** hedge, **the** principle of the thorn.   Cattle let it alone, and easily come **to** respect fence boundaries.

ADAPTATION TO THE SOUTH.

The general facts and principles, both of law and custom, which we **have** shown to belong to the fence system in the Southern states, derive fresh interest **and** meaning from the changes now making rapid progress in subdivision of lands.   The former large ownerships of impoverished and wasting land, **are** being strikingly replaced by a multitude of small possessions.   The effect **of** this could but be, and has already been proven to be, a stronger rivalry and a better tillage of these smaller areas.   In Mississippi, for instance, there **were** 42,840 plantations in 1860, and the average number of acres in each **was** 370.   There were in 1867 but 412 farms of less than ten acres ; only **2,314** of over ten and less than twenty acres, in 1870 there were 8,981 ; only 16,024 between twenty and one hundred acres, and in 1870, there were 8,981 ; only 16,024 between twenty and one hundred acres, and in 1870 there were 38,015.   Thus there was in this one state, a gain of nearly forty thousand **small** farms of less than one hundred acres in about three years.   **In** 1870 there were 68,023 farms the average area of each being 193 acres.   **In** 1880 the number **of** farms was 75,205, averaging 185 acres each, and **while** the nominal area **of** cultivated land in Mississippi **is less than it** was in 1860, the production is **twice** as great.

In Georgia the number **of** farms **cut off from the large plantations** from **1868 to** 1873 was 12,824.   In Liberty County there were **in** 1866 only three **farms** of less than **ten acres** ; in 1870 there **were** 616, and 749 farms between ten and twenty **acres.**   In Georgia **the small** colored **farmer owns** 680,000 acres of land cut **up into** farms that barely average ten acres each ; and in the Cotton States the **same** class owns 2,680,800 acres similarly divided.

Patent Galvanized Twisted Steel Wire Fencing. Without Barbs.

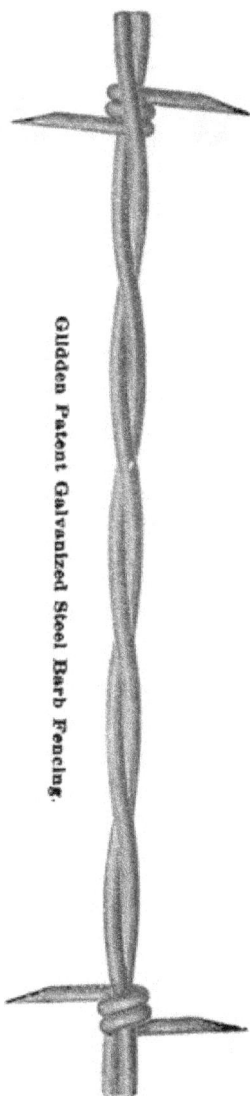

Glidden Patent Galvanized "THICKSET" Steel Barb Fencing.

Glidden Patent Galvanized Steel Barb Fencing.

But we are able to present official statistics to sustain our views. The following is Census Bulletin No. 262, showing statistics of the number and size of farms in the states of Alabama, Arkansas, Delaware, Florida, Georgia and South Carolina, according to the census of 1880.

THE NEW FARM SYSTEM OF THE SOUTH.

DEPARTMENT OF THE INTERIOR, CENSUS OFFICE,

Washington, D. C., September 10, 1881.

The following statistics, exhibiting the number and size of farms in six of the Southern States, are published as a Bulletin: first, for the earlier information of the people of the states concerned; and, second, as indicating the scope of the investigation into this subject in the present census.

Table I gives the gross number of farms, in each of the states referred to, in 1880, in comparison with the corresponding figures in 1870, 1860, and 1850.

Table II exhibits the distribution of this gross number of farms among three classes, viz. those cultivated by owners, those cultivated by occupiers who pay fixed money rentals, and those cultivated by occupiers who pay as rent a share of the produce. The information contained in this table has not been gathered at any preceding census.

Table III exhibits the distribution of the gross number of farms by classes according to acreage.

The marked feature of these tables is the immense increase in the number of farms in the states treated of, owing to the subdivision of the large plantations of twenty and thirty years ago, except only in the case of Delaware, where no very marked industrial change has occurred recently. In this state the increase of the number of farms only corresponds to the increase of population.

In Arkansas and Florida the increase in the number of farms is also partly accounted for by the occupation of considerable regions which were practically unsettled in 1870. To no small extent this result is due to immigration into these states.

FRANCIS A. WALKER,

Superintendent of Census.

TABLE I.—GROSS NUMBER OF FARMS.

	STATES.	1880.	1870.	1860.	1850.
1	Alabama, . . .	135,864	67,382	55,128	41,964
2	Arkansas, . . .	94,433	49,424	39,004	17,758
3	Delaware, . . .	8,749	7,615	6,658	6,063
4	Florida, . . .	23,438	10,241	6,568	4,304
5	Georgia, . . .	138,626	69,956	62,003	51,759
6	South Carolina, . .	93,864	51,889	33,171	29,967

TABLE II.—TENURE.

	STATES.	OWNER.	Rents for fixed money rental	Rents for shares of the produce
1	Alabama, . . .	72,215	28,888	40,761
2	Arkansas, . . .	65,245	9,916	19,272
3	Delaware, . . .	5,041	511	3,197
4	Florida, . . .	16,198	3,548	3,692
5	Georgia, . . .	76,451	18,557	43,618
6	South Carolina, . .	46,645	21,974	25,245

TABLE III.—DISTRIBUTION OF THE GROSS NUMBER OF FARMS, BY CLASSES, ACCORDING TO ACREAGE, OF LAND IMPROVED AND UNIMPROVED.

STATES.	Under 3 Acres.	3 and under 10.	10 and under 20.	20 and under 50.	50 and under 100.	100 and under 500.	500 and under 1000.	1000 and over.
1 Alabama,	277	3,597	18,055	41,721	26,447	44,254	4,645	1,868
2 Arkansas,	97	2,070	10,780	19,282	21,787	37,976	1,798	648
3 Delaware,	4	311	484	1,205	2,069	4,681	66	9
4 Florida,	69	1,301	2,456	7,640	4,381	6,562	652	377
5 Georgia,	101	3,110	8,694	36,524	26,054	53,635	7,017	3,491
6 South Carolina,	118	7,085	12,519	27,517	18,612	27,735	3,688	1,635

TABLE IV.—DISTRIBUTION, BY CLASSES, ACCORDING TO ACREAGE, OF FARMS OCCUPIED BY THEIR OWNERS.

STATES.	Under 3 Acres.	3 and under 10.	10 and under 20.	20 and under 50.	50 and under 100.	100 and under 500.	500 and under 1000.	1000 and over.
1 Alabama,	92	956	1,652	8,501	16,282	38,814	4,194	1,724
2 Arkansas,	33	585	1,417	8,981	18,135	33,962	1,561	571
3 Delaware,	3	243	325	799	1,223	2,411	32	5
4 Florida,	53	815	1,238	3,582	3,461	6,132	607	360
5 Georgia,	35	906	1,353	6,605	14,401	43,505	6,392	3,254
6 South Carolina,	34	1,168	2,609	5,914	8,750	23,358	3,276	1,536

Table V.—Distribution, by Classes, according to Acreage, of Farms Occupied by Persons Paying Rent at a Fixed Value in Money.

STATES.	Under 3 Acres.	3 and under 10.	10 and under 20.	20 and under 50.	50 and under 100.	100 and under 500.	500 and under 1000.	1000 and over.
1 Alabama,	51	1,058	3,251	11,858	3,995	2,343	248	84
2 Arkansas,	8	414	2,563	3,464	1,417	1,848	145	57
3 Delaware,	...	87	73	90	124	183	3	1
4 Florida,	6	262	582	1,980	452	236	24	6
5 Georgia,	27	978	1,631	8,205	3,616	3,680	280	140
6 South Carolina,	46	4,418	5,096	8,443	1,866	1,811	225	69

Table VI.—Distribution, by Classes, according to Acreage, of Farms Occupied by Persons Paying Rent in Shares of the Produce.

STATES.	Under 3 Acres.	3 and under 10.	10 and under 20.	20 and under 50.	50 and under 100.	100 and under 500.	500 and under 1000.	1000 and over.
1 Alabama,	134	1,583	8,152	21,362	6,170	3,097	203	60
2 Arkansas,	56	1,071	6,800	6,837	2,235	2,166	87	20
3 Delaware,	1	31	86	316	692	2,037	31	3
4 Florida,	10	224	636	2,128	468	194	21	11
5 Georgia,	39	1,226	5,710	21,714	8,037	6,450	345	97
6 South Carolina,	38	1,449	4,814	13,160	2,996	2,566	192	30

The census of 1870 will, it is believed, show a still greater change in the domestic economy of the South by the division of land. Not to take issue with those who see a present tendency toward a rebunching of the small farms speculators or in the hands of large owners, even by such massing of ownership the process is not one of restoring the old plantations, but of managing or rental of the small farms, which are in many instances being cut into even smaller farms, and leased to small croppers with better results all round. An instance of this kind is told where a resident of Oglethorpe, Georgia, a corn raiser, bought a place of 370 acres for $1,700; he at once put six tenants on it, and limited their cotton acreage to one-third of what they had under cultivation. Each of the six made more clear money than the former owner had made, and the rents for the first year were $1,126. The same owner has fifteen farms all run on the same plan.

This better cultivation is telling wonderfully on the increased production of cotton on the worn out lands of the olden Southern States, where the production of cotton has nearly doubled in the last decade, the increase far outstripping the increase of population; the greatest specific increase being in the Atlantic cotton states.

The cotton belt of the Atlantic States runs through generally a healthy country, with a salubrious climate, where an industrial population from any part of the globe can live and enjoy as good health as is accorded to man in other agricultural sections, and where they can raise, in addition to cotton, the cereals, roots and fruits.

What suggestion has ever been made of the utilities of the fenced possession of land, that does not most strongly apply to this very region, where the land owner has the benefit of his acres all the year round, and to get the best advantage of his soil needs to have at all seasons a PERFECT PROTECTION AGAINST ALL THE ENEMIES OF HIS CROPS.

Wood is scarce, and its use for fencing costly and wasteful, though this wastefulness has not yet come be appreciated by all farmers of the South and Southwest. Thus it is told that, while economists and thoughtful men in the older states are gravely discussing the problem of the coming timber famine, the Missouri farmers are splitting magnificent walnut, butternut, cherry and mulberry trees into common rails, for the inclosure of land.

A SPECIAL SOUTHERN FEATURE.

We come now to consider, with a purpose of deliberation and care, one special adaptation of Barb Fencing to the South. And here we shall present facts not our own, but derived from the study and experience of those who will be accepted as well known and accredited authorities as to Southern needs, and the possibilities of Southern industries and husbandry. Some of the best talent and practical far reaching experience of the time has been devoted to the question of Sheep Husbandry in the Southern States. Not a new question, save in some of its newer phases that are justly coming into prominence. Let us bring together from sources entitled to the highest respect, some of the prominent facts of our wool industries from the Southern standpoint, taking as our authority the excellent work of Hon. John L. Hayes in his *National Bulletin of Woolen Manufacturers*, and his admirable treatise *Sheep Husbandry at the South* (Boston 1878), prepared at the request of representative Southern men; also the sterling contribution to this branch of inquiry, by Commissioner Killibrew of Tennessee*, and other treatises and papers to be mentioned in their place.

It has become a common phrase that profitable sheep husbandry is synonymous with profitable farming, and that good sheep raising makes good farms, and both the husbandman and his farm rich. The incentive to sheep raising

---

*SHEEP HUSBANDRY. *A Work prepared for the farmers of Tennessee.* By J. B. Killibrew, A. M., Ph. D. Commissioner of Agriculture, Statistics, and Mines for the State of Tennessee, Nashville, 1880.

for wool is furnished in the fact that, with three and thirty millions of sheep in the United States, producing annually 100,000,000 pounds of wool, the annual consumption of wool by the entire population of the United States is estimated at six pounds per head, thus requiring the supply of three hundred million pounds of wool, or three times our present product. And inasmuch as each sheep averages two pounds of wool, this calls for the yield of one hundred and fifty million sheep. Here, therefore, is the cause for our present annual importation of forty millions of dollars worth of foreign wool, besides twenty millions of dollars worth of foreign made woolen goods, the larger part of which should be saved to American home industry.

The United States possess one-half the cheap fertile lands included in the wool zone of the world; nearly half her territory lies within it. Experience has amply proved that sheep are healthy in every part of the United States. And no section of the United States presents so many advantages for the successful raising of sheep as the country lying between the Atlantic and the Mississippi, between the Gulf of Mexico and the line drawn east and west at the head of Lake Michigan. Of this section the best portion lies south of the Ohio river.

For this there are some incontrovertible reasons established by modern science, and confirmed by far reaching experience. While sheep require a dry soil, and, as they naturally belong to mountain regions, a broken and varied surface best agrees with them, certain other climate facts are needed for their best condition and development as fleece bearers. The time has gone by when it was said and believed that wool growing was impossible in the South. It has been established that the fibre of wool is not changed or enlarged by climate. Both qualities of length of fibre and fineness are on the contrary greatly favored by the propitious climate of the South, whose superb fleeces have repeatedly carried away the premiums of the best markets of the world. Says Mr. Hayes:

Having examined the volume of awards of the exhibition at London of 1851, commonly called the World's Fair, we find that the report of the juries recognize the German wools as the finest and longest. Two prize medals of the same grade given to the German exhibitors were awarded to exhibitors from the United States. The awards are arranged in the order of merit. The first is given to Mr. Cockerill. It says: "The wool transmitted by the exhibitor of Nashville is well got up; and exhibits, like the preceding specimens (the German), a quality of fibre indicative of care and skill in the development and improvement of the fleece, which calls for the award of the prize medal." The report further says: "One of the able experts, whose valuable aid to the jury have already acknowledged, reports, 'Those shown by America (United States) as most approximating to the character of German wools.'"—*Sheep Husbandry in the South*, p. 12.)

It is now ascertained beyond discussion, that the exact remarkable conditions that create the American cotton belt, equally favor wool production.

This cotton belt, commencing in North Carolina, averaging two hundred miles in width, excepting where it ascends the Mississippi four hundred miles from its mouth, and terminating almost in a point in Southern Texas, has an axis whose mean temperature is 64°, with extremes from 27° by 30° to 98° by 104°.

The cotton plant seems to be in a peculiar manner dependent upon the latent moisture of the atmosphere supplied by the great volumes of vapor from the Gulf of Mexico, drawn inland by the draught of summer heat. The sheep herder finds within the same influence all the security against droughts that, in some seasons, are the dread and source of disaster in most of the other famous sheep growing regions of the world.

Again, the most successful sheep breeders of the South ascribe their success to the provision for their sheep of succulent food throughout the year. And this is furnished to a like degree in no other sheep raising region of the world. One of the most marked advantages of the South is the ability to grow grasses which may be pastured in winter. The native crab grass, which everywhere springs up in the stubble after the small grains have been harvested, and the Japan clover rapidly taking possession of uncultivated places in South Carolina and other states, are highly relished and a good pasture for sheep, while the Bermuda grass and other luxuriant and strong growths, long considered the pests of the plantation, have come to be highly appreciated by the best cultivators of the South. Of the Bermuda grass, which though not a winter grass is the best of all Southern grasses, Dr. Little the State Geologist of Georgia says :

"When the value of Bermuda grass is appreciated by farmers, and the thin and waste portion of their farms are clothed with it, which seems to have been intended especially for sheep, Georgia will sustain a sheep to every acre of territory, and 37,000,000 of sheep would be worth to their owners in the aggregate $37,000,000, net, per annum,—nearly double the present gross value of the cotton crop of the state."

Mr. C. W. Howard, himself a practical farmer of Georgia, and other writers, have declared the fitness of the South for the successful cultivation of valuable grasses ; though, as in all countries, there are portions of the South where grass will not grow. By aid of winter grasses it is perfectly practicable throughout a large portion of the South to raise sheep without other cost than interest on the land, and the value of the salt.

Dismissing, as we may safely do at this point, the general food question in Southern sheep raising, as thus being too strongly established to be disputed, we pass to the most important of agricultural questions now being presented in the South, and by her own leading minds,

THE RELATION OF WOOL GROWING TO THE COTTON CROP,

which promises, in the language of another, " to enthrone Queen Wool beside King Cotton." It is not necessary to reassert the ground frequently taken and most strongly by Southern men, that wool growing at the South is far more profitable than cotton culture, and involves far less labor, though it calls for unremitting attention. Many, indeed, of the most intelligent men of the South believe that the exclusive cultivation of cotton has been a scourge, instead of a blessing, to their country ; that in one state, Georgia, with a crop over 500,000 bales of cotton (worth, at 15 cents a pound, $75 per bale), its agricultural population, as a whole, were poorer at the end than at the beginning of the year ; that labor on a cotton plantation where a fall crop is planted, is without intermission and that it is excessive in the quantity required, often exceeding in cost the whole salable value of the plantation.

Says Mr. Howard of Georgia, before quoted :

"More than thirty years ago, the writer, walking with a gentleman of far-reaching mind, and observing the gullied and excoriated condition of the soil near Milledgeville, inquired : ' What is to restore its fertility to the worn out portion of Georgia ?' The answer was promptly given : 'Sheep and Bermuda grass.' There was profound wisdom in the reply. A large portion of old Georgia must become a sheep-walk, before it can be restored to fertility, and the land-owners realize the full benefits of their land."

" Mr. Robert C. Humber, of Putnam County, in Middle Georgia, keeps one hundred and thirty-eight sheep, of the cross between the merino and the common sheep. He says they cost nothing, except the salt they eat ; while they pay one hundred per cent. on the investment, in mutton, lambs and wool. They yield an average of three pounds of wool per head, which he sells at the very low price of twenty-five cents,—less than the market price. It costs him nothing, except the shearing. His sheep range on Bermuda grass,—old fields in summer, and the plantation at large, embracing the fields from which crops have been gathered, and the cane bottoms in winter."

J. H. Moore of Oakley, Arkansas, an experienced sheep breeder, commenced sheep raising in 1854, and wintered entirely with cotton seed and what grass the sheep could get in the cotton fields, **and**, with interruptions growing out of the war, has continued the practice **always** with success. Here is a leaf from his experience :

In 1879 I had 31 ewes, which were wintered during last winter entirely on **cotton seed. They** dropped 53 lambs, of which I saved 47. I fed these more seed, as I had plenty, and **fed on the** ground, which caused the waste of nearly one-half the seed. Cotton seed can be purchased **at** the gins at from three to four dollars per ton of 2,000 pounds. One ton will winter from **10 to** 15 sheep when fed on the ground ; if fed in troughs, it would winter 20 to 30 sheep.

I suppose the seed must be good feed, as the sheep look well. A neighbor of mine, who was a large sheep-breeder in Ohio, says that one ton to forty sheep is enough when they have the run of the pasture, and that he can winter well a sheep at ten cents per head.

There are many plantations in the South that are too much worn to make the cultivation of cotton profitable, that could be brought to their original fertility by feeding sheep with cotton seed on the field. These plantations could be divided into four fields, **one** of which could **be set** to Bermuda grass, which will afford grazing for as many sheep as eight **or ten** per acre as long as it would be healthy to keep them on it ; one field be sown with cow-pease, and fed **off** the ground during the winter ; and, after the pease and vines were consumed, the sheep could be fed on the field the balance of the winter on cotton seed, and their droppings, together with manure from the pea-vine, would double the crop of cotton ; and by this means the planter would enrich his land and himself at same time.

I find Bermuda grass as good grazing as any I have ever tried ; but it is only a summer grass, and seems to do best during hot dry weather, but requires to be kept closely grazed, as it gets hard when old ; but this could be remedied by keeping cattle and sheep in alternate pastures.

My experience teaches me that sheep can be wintered in the South at a cost of ten to fifteen cents per head, and, if credit be given them for the weeds and briers they destroy, and the land they manure, the cost is less than nothing. Another profit could **be** added to sheep husbandry at the South, and that is *the increased value of worn-out cotton plantations, which might be computed at ten per cent. on the original* **cost** *of the land.*

Says Mr. Hayes, (*Sheep Husbandry in the South*) :

"A **most** important branch of sheep husbandry, in its relations to the improvement of a country, *is that where the culture of sheep is made auxiliary to a mixed husbandry   The highest advantage of this system is the improvement of the land.*

"Sheep are the only animals which do not exhaust the land upon which they feed, but permanently improve it. Horned cattle, especially cows in milk, by continued grazing, ultimately exhaust the pastures of their phosphates. In England, the pastures of the county of Chester, famous as a cheese district, are kept up only by the constant use of bone dust. Sheep, on the other hand, through the peculiar nutritiousness of their manure, and the facility with which it is distributed, are found to be *the most economical and certain means of constantly renewing the productiveness of the land.* By the combination of sheep husbandry with wheat culture, lands in England, which, in the time of Elizabeth, produced on an average, six and a half bushels of wheat per acre, produce now over thirty bushels. For these reasons, the recent practical writers in the Journal of the Royal Agricultural Society of England, pronounce that, while there is no profit in growing sheep in England simply for their mutton and wool, sheep husbandry is still an indispensable necessity, as the sole means of keeping up the land.

"Experience in the United States leads to similar conclusions. Mr. Stilson of Wisconsin, by keeping sheep, is able to raise his twenty-four bushels of wheat to the acre, while the average yield of wheat in Wisconsin is but **ten** bushels. There are cases in Vermont where sheep-farmers have been compelled to abandon one farm after another, as they became too fertile for profitable sheep-growing.

"The farmers of Connecticut in former times, it would appear, had a full appreciation of the fertilizing influences of the sheep. In the town of Goshen, in Connecticut, according to my informant, the public roads were anciently laid out eight rods wide ; and in these roads it was the custom to pasture in common the sheep belonging to the individual proprietors of the town, which were taken care of by a man and a boy, at the expense of the town authorities. The yarding of the sheep for each night, in order that the benefits of the manure might not be lost, was let out at the town meeting. On the evening of the 27th of May, just preceding the famous cold summer of 1816, it came to the turn of a certain farmer to yard the sheep for the night. He had no field fenced which would hold the sheep,—some eight hundred in number,—except a field planted with corn, which had already come up. Preferring to sacrifice the corn to losing the manure, he turned the flock into this very field. On that night the frost cut off all the corn in the town, and the sheep had cut off our farmer's, who congratulated himself, in the morning, that he was no worse off than his neighbors. He soon found that he was better off. The sheep by cutting of the top shoots had saved the plants from being killed by the frost, and the droppings from the sheep in one night had so enriched the field that it produced the largest crop of corn that had been grown in the town for years."

Says Mr. Howard, in his excellent paper on the condition of Agriculture in the Cotton States, giving his own practical tests on Georgia lands :

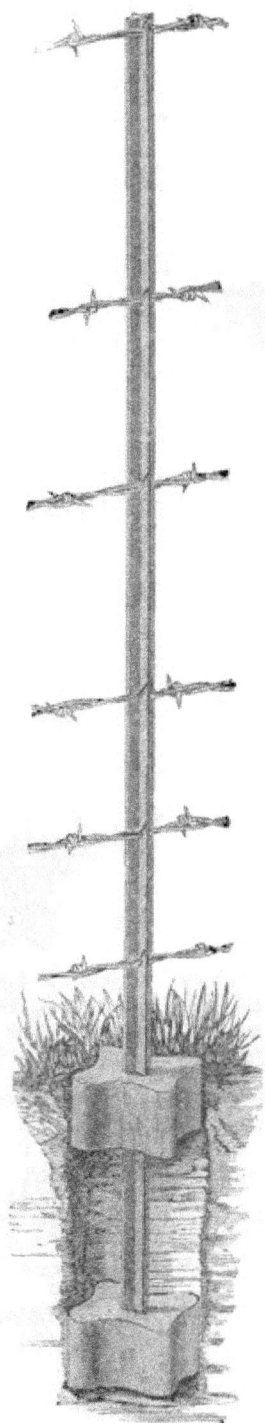

" It is by far the cheapest method of manuring land. No hauling manure is required, as the sheep haul their own manure, both solid and liquid, to precisely the spot on which it is desired to apply it. It is evenly spread, without labor, no part being excessively manured at the expense of another part. The effect of this manuring will be felt for years. Land so manured is good for two bags of cotton to the acre the following year. The other advantage is the fine condition into which the sheep are put at a season of the year when mutton brings the highest price. When land is put into sufficiently good order to bring five hundred bushels of turnips to the acre, the gain in mutton is equivalent to the cost of the crop. The heavy manuring of the land is, then, clear gain."

Sheep manure, from its coldness, does not ferment like horse dung, and therefore retains its value much longer than the excrement of the horse or man. It ranks among the very best of the manures produced by animals, especially from those sheep that are fed with rich food for fattening purposes. As has been already stated, mastication of sheep is so perfect there is no danger of weed seeds coming up after having passed through the stomach of a sheep. Both the urine and the dung are very rich in fertilizing properties. Urea, the active principle of urine, has a large quantity of nitrogen in it, and sheep's urine contains, according to one of our best analysts, 28 parts of urea in every 1,000 parts, and 12 parts of salt, among which is a large proportion of phosphoric acid. In one hundred parts of the dung of sheep there are 68 per cent. of water, 19.3 of animal and vegetable matter, and 12.7 per cent. of saline matters. This 19.3 per cent. of organic matter contains as much nitrogen, which is the value of manures chiefly, as 43 parts of horse dung, 63 parts of hog manure, or 125 parts of cow dung, and is equal to 100 parts of the ordinary stable or barnyard manure. It is much drier than other manures, having but little water, comparatively speaking. For instance, let a horse receive 100 parts of dry fodder, and he will defecate 216 pounds of fresh manure, which being dried, makes 46 pounds of dry manure, while the sheep with the same food would give but 128 pounds of fresh manure, making 43 pounds of dried. This is manure made with the ordinary method of feeding, such as hay, fodder, and such grass as they can pick up. But when sheep are fed with grain or other highly stimulating food for fattening purposes, with food rich in albumen and phosphates, the oil and starch only are assimilated and go to the formation of fat and flesh, while the remainder, including the larger part of the salts, goes to the manure heap, thus adding very greatly to its value as a land application. This fact has long been known and used to the improvement of land by the English farmer, and must be learned and practiced by our people. The declining fertility of our soils call loudly for all the aid we can give it, and it is time to recognize the fact that, if we continue to draw from the land, and never put anything to it, it will after awhile cease to respond to our calls upon it. (*Killibrew's Sheep Husbandry.*)

The *Journal of the American Agricultural Association* contains a very careful Canadian computation on this point. It says the enclosures may be arranged to accommodate a certain number of sheep, so that the land may be properly and regularly manured. The calculation is that one sheep passing one night on one square yard of land is equal, in money value, to £3, 10s. ($17.50) per acre; and it is upon this basis that acts of husbandry, as they are called, for which the incoming tenant has to pay his predecessor, are valued. Says this writer:

"Think, for a moment, of what passes in the fold during the night. The land has been recently ploughed ; the liquid and solid dejections are therefore easily absorbed, the oil from the fleece forming by no means an inappreciable part of them. The sheep, many weighing from a hundred and twenty pounds each, pass eight or ten hours on the same spot, and the pressure of their bodies, together with the trampling of their tiny-pointed hoofs, condense and solidify the land in a fashion that no roller, not even Crosskill's clod crusher, could hope to emulate."

The presence of five hundred sheep upon a Southern farm will it is declared enrich five acres every month in the year far better than purchased fertilizers, and at the same time pay in wool and mutton a better per cent than does cotton upon the labor and expense. Col. Watts of Laurens Co., South Carolina, a life-long sheep breeder in South Carolina, Georgia and Texas, keeps at the rate of one thousand sheep to the acre, which he regards as equivalent to four hundred pounds of the best guano. Its effects are perceptible for several years. He believes, from careful experimenting, that fifty-two acres of land can be so well fertilized in twelve months, by one thousand sheep, as to be rich soil for five years following. He declares the effects of such manuring wonderful. We might go on with these citations far beyond all reasonable limits, and yet not exhaust the statement of a fact known to American sheep breeders. We are now to speak of the relations that are coming to be considered, between Wool growing and Cotton raising. And here we bring forward from Hon. Edward Atkinson some of the points presented in his address at Atlanta, Ga., Oct., 1880.

COTTON AND WOOL IN THE SAME FIELD.

We do not attempt to present his elaborate argument in full, but our selection will show his view of comparative results :

" Assuming good cultivation and an average product of 400 pounds lint, there will be from 1,050 to 1,250 pounds of seed to each acre on the average. After setting aside enough selected seed for planting, there will be 1,000 pounds left for feeding.

It is the production of seed that exhausts the soil, and not of fibre. In the four hundred pounds lint there are but four pounds of chemical elements drawn from the soil ; but in the thousand pounds of seed there are forty pounds of phosphate of lime and potash.

If this seed is used for a fertilizer as it comes from the gin, it works slowly and unevenly. The oil injures it as a fertilizer. It should all be fed to stock in order to give the best results.

It seems to suit sheep well if fed whole ; but, for hogs and cattle, the more the oil is removed, the better it is.

Now let us see what may be done on the basis of ascertained facts.

Each 400 acres can be surrounded by a FIVE-ROW, BARBED-WIRE, DOG-PROOF FENCE, and divided into four fields by cross fences at a cost, including posts and setting, of less than a thousand dollars.

In each 400 acres let one field be devoted to corn, one to cow-pease, one to cotton, and one to sheep. The seed from a first product of 200 pounds of cotton per acre with the grass which follows the cotton, would carry two and a half sheep per acre on the next field for six months ; and the cow-pease and the corn-fodder would serve for the rest of the year. The pea-vines and sheep dung would increase the crop, and more sheep would be added each year, until, in the third or fourth year the average would be 400 pounds cotton per acre on 100 acres, five sheep per acre on one hundred acres, a corn crop increased in the same proportion as the cotton, say from ten to 15 bushels to an acre to 20 or 30 bushels on the third 100 acres, and the cow-pease to be ploughed in, or Bermuda grass to be cropped by sheep, on the fourth 100 acres.

Let us assume the conditions and cost on a moderate scale, so that the undertaking may **not** seem so visionary as the large figures given in the preceding.

A farm to be purchased consisting of rather poor sandy soil. **This I assume can be had at less** than five dollars per acre.

Say 500 acres at.... ....$2,500
Fencing and dividing 400 acres with barbed wire fence............ 1,000
Barn and sheds in center of the quadrangle, including gin-stand and **other appliances**.... 1,000
Tools and implements. 500

Total............... ....$5,000

Houses **according to circumstances, and five hundred sheep at a price conditioned on their** quality

It may be assumed that ten thousand dollars would be an ample capital for such a beginning ; but these figures are based on theory, and not on practice. Perhaps a much less sum would serve the purpose.

One thing more may be considered in this connection. While it is doubtless true that sheep thrive on the whole cotton seed with the oil in it, yet it appears that there is too much oil. It affects the milk of the breeding ewes, and also deposits a great excess of grease in the fleece.

It would be truer economy to extract all the oil that can be removed by pressure, and then the ground cake and hulls would be in true condition to feed to sheep, cattle, or hogs.

Machines for hulling the seed can now be purchased at moderate cost ; and we may be very sure that, as soon as a demand for small presses for farm use is made, the supply will come. The Dederick hay-press is now being used for packing cotton fibre to a compression equal to the density of elm wood, or forty pounds to a cubic foot, and the inventor of that press seems equal to any emergency.

The removal of the oil, like the removal of the fibre, takes almost nothing from the land devoted to cotton, the mineral element being about three-fourths in the kernel and one-fourth in the hull.

This suggestion is one of a class inviting attention to the special features and great promise of a mode of sheep raising suited to the South, and needed for her people and their lands. It is not a new proposition. In North Carolina the farmers have practised grazing their sheep upon their fields of small grain during the winter "which," says a careful writer : " when judiciously done, rather contributes to than deteriorates from their yield at harvest."

This, then, is the statement from some of the leading industrial writers of the day, of the best possibilities of Southern husbandry, sufficiently attractive when thus given, and still more so when carefully compared with abundant testimony, to awaken the enthusiasm of every one who is interested in the development of the South.

Sheep husbandry is a rich mine of wealth, best developed alongside the cotton crop, giving a larger yield of best wool, advancing continually the fertility

of the soil, and *all this is made possible by a suitable system of fencing*. For
such fencing is required a material light of weight, easily constructed, or easily
changed from place to place, as the fields and feeding places are changed in
constant rotation. What other material meets these conditions but Barb
Wire Fencing, which, as before shown, is so largely replacing all other kinds
of fence material, both for permanent and transient fences?

THE PROTECTION OF BARB FENCING.

But we are further to discuss a need and a benefit pertaining to Barb Fencing, applicable to no other fence ; and this need is derived from the consideration of facts of the present and past sheep husbandry in the South, in
relation to one of its most serious deterring features.

The reports of the very able statistician of the Department of Agriculture,
which, from a careful examination of the system adopted by him in arriving
at results, we regard as very reliable, show the number of sheep in the South.

Number of Sheep in Southern States, January, 1878.

STATES.	Number of sheep.
Delaware	35,000
Maryland	151,200
Virginia	422,000
North Carolina	490,000
South Carolina	175,000
Georgia	382,300
Florida	56,500
Alabama	270,000
Mississippi	250,000
Louisiana	125,000
Texas	3,674,700
Arkansas	285,000
Tennessee	850,000
West Virginia	549,900
Kentucky	900,000
Missouri	1,271,000
Total	9,887,6000

Now no fact is more prominent among those gathered from this great industry
than

THE SHEEP-KILLING DOG A PERIL.

Legislatures have not found it easy to overcome or repress the friendship that
exists between the dog owner and his four-footed favorite, even if the former
be in the depths of poverty himself, and his pet a worthless cur with no other
merit than the affectionate wag of his tail. North Carolina Courts have declared the dog a wild beast, to be shot at sight if found trespassing. Many
sheep breeders have, with their quick shots, been a law to themselves on this
matter, but the nights are long, and the prowling sheep eaters numerous.
This evil is graphically stated by Commissioner Killibrew of Tennessee.

The country is often in an uproar from the depredations of one or two miserable curs in a
single night. The farmer goes to bed proud of being possessed of a fine nucleus of a flock. He
has carefully selected choice breeds, and spent many anxious hours protecting and caring for
them through the winter months, and it is his delight to exhibit them to his neighbors. But
some morning the unwelcome word comes to him, "the dogs have been among the sheep."
Every one who has experienced it knows of the volume of rage that swell his bosom. But it is
all for naught. The mischief is done, and the robber gone. Not a trace is left, except the dead
carcasses of many sheep lying around, and the frightened, stunned look of the more fortunate
ones that have escaped—escaped the dogs it may be, but they have suffered so much by fear they
do not recover for months. They run at the approach of any one, they are restless, and the constant about of some watcher startles them from their food, and, as a consequence, they lose flesh
and become a shadow of what they were before. Sheep are very peculiar in this respect, and
nothing disturbs their equanimity more than the inroads of dogs. No animal is more easily

gentled than a sheep, and none thrive more by it. If dogs are allowed to go near them, and they are continually frightened, they will become so demoralized they will actually suffer from hunger while the troughs are full.

The Thirty-ninth General Assembly of Tennessee enacted a dog law, greatly to the relief and satisfaction of the sheep-raisers throughout the state. Many farmers who had hitherto been deterred from raising sheep, soon engaged in the enterprise, and many more were preparing to do so; but, before the good effects of the law were scarcely realized, the following Legislature (the 40th) repealed the law, it seems to the great disheartenment of the sheep-raisers At this juncture, and to ascertain public opinion and the sheep farmers' experience on this subject, the Commissioner of Agriculture sent out circulars of inquiry to all parts of the state of Tennessee. From the analysis of answers to these questions, Mr. Killibrew brings to light a discouraging item in the large number of sheep that have fallen a prey to the ruthless curs that prowl and growl and howl through his state. " A very cursory glance at the replies to the question as to the number of sheep annually destroyed by dogs will serve to show that not less than 7,000 are annually immolated upon the altar of caninal affection." Here are some of these replies :

Farmers' Testimony as to Annual Destruction of Sheep by Dogs.

Half a dozen farmers present estimate the number from 300 to 1,000.
About one-fifth annually.
Cannot give any estimate.
About 800, worth $1,600.
One-fourth.
None since the dog law was passed.
In the last three years but few, but previously one-fourth.
About one-half of the whole amount.
200 in this county. Must now increase.
500.
A great many, don't know the number.
Don't know, less the past season than ever.
About one-fourth.
About 25 per cent. of the whole.
50 sheep valued at $62.50.
About 10 per cent.
About 1,000, value $3,000.
5 per cent.
100 head.
10 per cent.
About 200 or 300.
500.
Very few.
About $12,000.
About $5,000.
$15,000 to $20,000.
$7,000 or $8,000.

Some say if it were not for dogs they would go into the business.
Very few since the dog law was passed.
One-half to three-fourths of the whole number.
10 to 20 per cent.
10 per cent.
Not less than 20 per cent.
10 to 15 per cent.
$2,500 in value.
10 per cent.
About 10 per cent.
About one-fourth.
25 per cent., valued at $15,500.
A very considerable number.
100, value $125.
1,000 for this county.
About 10 per cent.
Cannot answer, know it to be large.
Cannot give the number, think it great.
Very considerable.
Very few while the dog law was in force.
About one-third of the whole; 300 to 500 a year.
$10,000.
$12,000.
Yes, quite a number.
It prevents many from following it as an occupation.

Says J. W. F. Foster, in discussing sheep husbandry in East Tennessee :

THE DOG, more than any other one thing, is keeping East Tennessee poor. If, according to the Spanish proverb, beneath the foot of the sheep is prosperity and wealth, beneath that of the dog is decay and poverty. From data furnished by the assessment rolls, we have in this division of the state at least sixty thousand dogs If, before the tribunal of Reason and Common Sense, an indictment were preferred against these dogs as a public nuisance, such an array of charges could be made and sustained as would insure a verdict of guilty, and with scarcely any palliating circumstances for an appeal to the mercy of the court. It would be proved that the food consumed by each dog would produce one hundred and fifty pounds of pork, which would aggregate nine million pounds, worth, at the lowest estimate, five hundred and forty thousand dollars. It would be shown that the destruction of property by them annually averages but little less than that produced by fire and flood. It would be shown that, in consequence of their evil disposition, our farmers are deterred from engaging in the raising of sheep, by which a loss of revenue is caused to the people and to the state of at least five millions of dollars annually. It would be shown that large numbers of immigrants, with money in their purses and brains in their heads, are prevented from settling among us and helping to build up the country, from the fact that these dogs render it too hazardous to embark in the only agricultural operation that offers a reasonable prospect of profit. It is a crime against the dignity and welfare of the State that such a nuisance should exist.

What better remedy or resort, after the law makers have done all they can or should do, to check this evil, than to make sure the safety at home by the judicious use of *a fence the dog cannot pass.* No other fence than Steel Barb Fencing meets this requisite. The sheep field and the sheep fold can be cheaply and securely made DOG PROOF. And it will be easy to erect light screens and feeders at close run ways, and in smaller pens, to prevent the barb from tearing the fleeces. Sheep breeders agree that with fences of common construction, the sheep huddle in their shade and shelter, at the borders of the field, making them even more a temptation and a prey to the dog. The light, strong Barb Fence has no shelter or shade to offer, and only one suggestion without and within—for all animals *to keep at a distance from it.*

IN CONCLUSION.

We have thus sought to review some of the general and particular facts of fencing and of the fence system in this country and the Southern States. The figures are striking in their magnitude, but are as authentic as any statistics of our domestic industries, and have been derived from sources beyond challenge for their accuracy. And yet their presentment is comparatively new, for it is only within a few years that the attention of national and state agricultural authorities has been turned to a careful view of the fence question. When it is stated that upwards of one hundred and twenty-five thousand miles of Barb Fencing has passed into use in the last few seasons, it may seem an extravagant assertion ; perhaps to be received with incredulity, as impossible. But the sum representing the total cost of fences in the United States, given in one of our first paragraphs, represents over SIX MILLION MILES of fences in use in the United States at the time of the government inquiry of 1871, and the same form of statement applied to the fence statistics of the Southern States, presented in the same connection, shows that, at that time, Kentucky had nearly THREE HUNDRED THOUSAND MILES of fences, and Tennessee nearly TWO HUNDRED THOUSAND miles. In the Iowa State Agricultural Report for 1863, a careful computation for that state alone showed nearly FOUR HUNDRED THOUSAND miles of fences. Compared with these substantial and authentic fence exhibits, the reader who may be fresh in this field of inquiry will be better able to appreciate the facts of Barb Fencing, and the era it opens. Let us briefly review some of the more obvious conclusions from what we have presented.

1 *We cannot do without fencing.* Old custom, and modern needs sustaining such custom, point to the suitable fencing of land as the only security to the profit, and peace of mind of the land owner. So largely has Barb Fencing been adopted to meet this need, that its statistics of manufacture are to-day among the most solid figures of the Wire industry, and of the hardware trade in farm supplies.

2. *Fencing is costly.* For the Fence, taken in the aggregate, the outlay is heavy, and under the old systems wasteful. What other direction of farm economy promises better and surer saving than Barb Fence, when cost and ease of construction and maintenance are considered ?

3. *The South has special needs for fencing.* All leading authorities, her own men, earnest to repair and build up her industries, are to day urging it with tongues and pens. How far Barb Fencing comes in naturally among the indispensable agencies of this reform, we have tried to show in these pages.

4. *The farmer's enemies are many.* He must protect his fields and his flocks. Barb fencing will help him to protect them.

5. *Defective legislation* exists in the South, which it is for her law-makers to repair, but the farmer cannot wait on the statute books, while his farm is running to waste, and the dogs are eating his sheep. He cannot take the law into his own hands, but he can stretch the impregnable line of law and order about his own premises, and no caucus or clique can make his Barb Fence otherwise than secure to everything within its protection.

6. *It is no experiment.* Barb Fence has to day a literally broader relation to the developement of American husbandry, and the enjoyment of land owning,

than any other material agency now before the public. It holds the herds to their pasture, and from the cultivated field. It protects life and property along the railway lines. It fixes the boundary as a barrier about the immense ranche. It makes secure against thieves, the small estate of the fruit grower and the raiser of choice crops. It defies the roving pig as a Southern institution, and the mutton stealing dog as the scourge of the flocks. It makes possible for the South the best rewards of mixed husbandry.

7. *It commends itself* to the largest land owner, with whom the cheapness of fence material is of the utmost importance. It meets the changed condition of Southern farms and landed properties, where multiplication of small land owners makes important the better maintenance of boundaries. To avoid complications and controversies, good fencing is a necessity. The tendency throughout the South and Southwest is to smaller farms, and better enclosures on large tracts. Even in Texas the former practice of free range is being abandoned. Contests were constantly occurring between the cattle-herders and the shepherds. Sheep breeders, therefore, began gradually to purchase all the lands required; and, at present, the greater part of the land in the sheep-region is held in freehold by the respective flock-masters. About fifty miles from Corpus Christi, in Nueces County, 80,000 acres are being enclosed in one vast pasture by a Barb Wire fence, at a cost of $16,000.

An incorporated company for sheep breeding has been formed in Southern Missouri, 150 miles from St. Louis. The incorporators propose to locate 30,000 acres of land on the side of the Ozark Mountains, and to start with 4,000 sheep fenced in at less cost than herdsmen can be employed. They expect to bring the land under cultivation at an early day, and to graze the sheep on blue and tame grass instead of on bunch grass; also to provide shelter and winter feed for the flocks, with other necessary improvements as needed. This is more sensible than the Colorado system, which relies on pasturing or starvation in the winter; and how fully does this apply to the present argument.

The traveller by the Atchison, Topeka, and Santa Fe Railroad is astonished to see running straight across the prairie from west to east, a short distance below Springer station, a Barb Wire Fence, which marks the Southern boundary of the famous Maxwell Grant, of New Mexico, of over one million acres, which is thus fenced in on the south and east, making the longest lines of continuous fence in the world, inclosing a pasture of *seven hundred thousand acres.* By this means the vast herds are kept on their owners' land, and other herds excluded. Including the inner inclosures for such separation of cattle as may be desired, there are upwards of two hundred miles of Barb Wire Fence on this Grant. Some of the inner inclosures are ten miles square. Let any one estimate the great saving of cost, on tracts of these magnitudes, by the use of Barb Fence, as compared with any other known fencing.

The history of the connection of the Washburn & Moen Manufacturing Company and I. L. Ellwood & Co. with the Barb Fencing may be briefly told. As the largest general wire manufacturers in this country, our works at Grove Street and Quinsigamond, in the city of Worcester, Mass., being the largest exclusively wire manufacturing establishment in the world, Washburn & Moen Manufacturing Company have for twenty-five years past had a broader and more intimate relation with fencing and fence topics than any and all other parties in this country. For many years after the first introduction of plain iron wire as fencing material, our works were among the largest sources of supply, our improved process of galvanizing having created a high character for our wire. On the introduction of the principle of arming the Wire with the Barb, we became principally instrumental in bringing together the various patents to produce a perfect product; also in the introduction by us of an entirely new class of automatic machinery for the manufacture of

Barb Fencing.   The Barb Wire Fence industry of this country is now represented by nearly fifty manufacturers—licensees under our patents.   The state-
ments brought together in these pages will not be understood as manufacturers' facts, but as public facts the manufacturers find **it their** interest to seek out
and bring together.   They will have only the weight deserved by the high
sources whence they are derived.

   Are these facts controvertible?   Can the same measure of benefit **be** reached
in any other way so cheaply, so well, and so thoroughly, as by the improved
system of fencing, herein suggested?   It will be for all, as practical men,
alive to their own interests, or as leaders of public thought and opinion, to an-
swer, after giving due weight to the facts brought together in these pages.

WASHBURN & MOEN M'F'G CO.

WORCESTER, MASS.

I. L. ELLWOOD & CO.

DE KALB, ILLS.

APPENDIX.

Statistics of Fences in the United States.

The following is from the U. S. Government Inquiry of 1871, the corresponding figures for the Southern States having been given in the body of this pamphlet:

Total Cost of Fences.

Maine	$31,214,606	Indiana	100,759,415
New Hampshire	34,525,227	Illinois	128,856,513
Vermont	42,929,880	Wisconsin	39,302,719
Massachusetts	36,916,283	Minnesota	6,539,037
Rhode Island	9,877,736	Iowa	34,729,338
Connecticut	33,801,950	Kansas	7,371,548
New York	228,874,611	Nebraska	2,174,020
New Jersey	40,496,513	California	25,598,298
Pennsylvania	179,834,494	Oregon	5,274,470
Ohio	153,580,673	Nevada	444,680
Michigan	57,441,104		

Average Cost of Fences.

	Cost per rod.		Cost per rod.		Cost per rod.
Maine	$1.00	New Jersey	1.60	Minnesota	$ .88
New Hampshire	1.20	Pennsylvania	1.15	Iowa	1.10
Vermont	1.33	Ohio	1.00	Kansas	1.00
Massachusetts	1.75	Michigan	.95	Nebraska	1.05
Rhode Island	2.20	Indiana	1.05	California	1.40
Connecticut	1.70	Illinois	1.20	Oregon	1.05
New York	1.35	Wisconsin	.85	Nevada	1.50

The Cost of Repairs.

The annual cost of repairs of fences varies with the cost of material of which they are constructed, and the durability of that material. It is lowest in the New England section on account of the large proportion of stone wall; and low in the South from cheapness of material; but in most of the older States, where timber is becoming scarce, and in the prairie states, which are nearly destitute of most supplies, the expense of repairs of fences is high, as well as in the sections where soft wood, brush and poles are extensively used.

The figures for repairs in the several states show a footing total of annual outlay of $93,636,187.

Total Annual Exhibit.

Total cost of annual repairs. $93,963,187
Interest on the original cost, at 6 per cent 104,852,985

Grand total, exclusive of re-building $198,816,172

The average cost of material is given in tables of states, which show that boards for fences are dearest in Texas, $29.53 per M.; $28.95 in Kansas; $27.88 in Nebraska; $27.00 in Delaware, and $5 66 in Rhode Island. The cost of rails ranges from $13 per M. in New Jersey, to $8.12 per M. in Florida.

The "Legal Fence" in the United States.

"All of the States have laws recognizing in some way the obligation to fence." (*Tyler's Law of Fences*, 504.) The height of the legal fence in the several states and territories varies as follows:

Four feet high—Maine, New Hampshire, Massachusetts, Delaware, Idaho and Washington.

Four and a half feet—Vermont, Rhode Island, Connecticut, New York. New Jersey, Maryland, West Virginia, Ohio, Michigan, Indiana, Illinois, Wisconsin. Minnesota, Iowa, Tennessee, Louisiana, Kansas, Nebraska, Colorado, Oregon, Arizona, Nevada, Montana, Dakota, Utah.

Five feet—Pennsylvania, Virginia, Missouri, Kentucky, North Carolina, Georgia, Alabama, South Carolina, Florida, Mississippi, Texas, Arkansas, California, Wyoming.

The following from the statutes of Southern States indicates The Legal Fence, as variously prescribed:

DELAWARE. (*Revised Code*, 1874, p. 285.) *Section* 1. A good fence of wood, stone, or well set thorn, four and a half feet high or four feet high, and having a ditch within two feet, shall be deemed a lawful fence in Newcastle and Kent Counties; and in Sussex County four feet shall be the height of lawful fences.

MARYLAND. There is no general fence law, but special laws exist for the several counties; for example, as follows: (*Laws of* 1870, *Chap.* 637.)

Baltimore County.—Fences sufficiently close to prevent hogs or pigs from passing through the same, or post and rail fence five feet high, not less than five rails in each panel.

Caroline County.—Outside fences of all grounds kept for enclosure, rail fences four and a half feet high, worm fences five feet high.

Anne Arundel County. The lawful fence, if of posts and rails, four feet high; if worm fence, five feet high.

VIRGINIA. (*Code* 1878, p. 780.) *Section* 1. Every fence five feet high; which, if the fence be on a mound shall include the mound to the bottom of the ditch, shall be deemed a lawful fence as to any of the stock named in the eighth section of this chapter which could not creep through the same.

Section 8. If any horses, cattle, hogs, sheep or goats shall enter into any grounds inclosed by a lawful fence, owners of such animals to be liable, etc. (*Laws of* 1860.)

(The "No Fence Law" of 1866, amended 1873, provides that the boundaries of all counties adopting the fence law of 1866 shall be declared lawful fence. Good and substantial gates to be erected in such enclosing fences at all crossings of public roads, where the court of the county shall require the same, the cost of such outer fences to be equitably distributed among all owners and occupants benefitted. Within such limits no domestic animals to be permitted to run at large, beyond limits of owner's land, under penalty of double damages, etc. This law to be repealed (Sec. 23) on the vote of three-fifths of the voters.)

NORTH CAROLINA. (*Rev. Stat.* 1873, p 425.) *Section* 1. Every planter shall make a sufficient fence about his cleared ground under cultivation, at least five feet high. (Navigable stream to be a sufficient fence.)

Sec. 2. (Enumerates rivers and streams that are sufficient fences.)

(The "No Fence Act" [Session laws 1872-3] provides that citizens of counties or townships may erect a good and substantial fence around their territory, with gates on all the public roads, where they enter into and pass out of its borders. Two or more townships may unite and put their territory under one common fence.)

SOUTH CAROLINA. (*Rev. Stat.* 1873, p. 296.) *Section* 1. All fences closely and strongly made, of rails, boards, posts and rails, or of an embankment of earth capped with rails and timber of any sort, or live hedges FIVE FEET high from surface of the earth, shall be deemed to be lawful fences ; and every planter shall be bound to keep such lawful fence around his cultivated grounds.

(The "No Fence Act," (*Extra Session* 1877.) When a majority of township electors in such town, or in any county, shall "desire to substitute the fencing of stock, in lieu of fencing of crops," commissioners of said county may erect fences along lines of such townships or counties, gates to be maintained at all highway crossings; a tax to be levied and collected upon property of such township or county, for the expense of such fences.)

GEORGIA. (*Code* 1873, p 244.) 1443. All fences or enclosures called worm fences, shall be FIVE FEET high, with or without being staked and ridered, and, from the ground to the height of three feet, the rails shall not be more than four inches apart. All paling fences shall be five feet from the ground, and the palings not more than two inches apart.

(The "No Fence Law of 1872 provides that in each and every county which shall, by vote, adopt its provisions, the GENERAL FENCE LAW is repealed, and all boundary lines shall be declared a lawful fence, and no animals in such counties, &c., allowed to run at large beyond limits of owner's lands.

1455. Provides for submitting above to counties for balloting—"Fence," or "No Fence," &c.)

ALABAMA. (*Session Laws* 1878-9, p. 75). All enclosures and fences must be at least FIVE FEET high, and if made of rails the rails not more than four inches apart from the ground to the height of every two feet; or, if made of palings, the palings to be not more than three inches apart, or if made with a ditch, such ditch must be made four feet wide at the top and the fence, of whatever material composed, at least five feet high from the bottom of the ditch, and three feet high from the top of the bank, so close as to prevent stock of any kind from getting through. *Provided,* that a rail fence FIVE FEET high, with rails not more than eighteen inches apart, from the ground to the height of every three feet, shall be a lawful fence so far as cattle, horses, and mules are concerned. (*Approved January,* 1879.)

MISSISSIPPI. (*Laws* 1871, p. 408.) 1905. All fences FIVE FEET high, substantially and closely built with planks, pickets, hedges, or other good material, and which are strong and close enough to exclude domestic animals of ordinary habits and disposition, are to be taken and considered as lawful fences, as long as they are kept in good repair.

(A fence made of common rails and built in the form known as worm fence to be SIX FEET high, and kept in good repair, is also a lawful fence.)

FLORIDA. (*Digest,* 1872.) *Section* 1. All fences or inclosures commonly called worm, log, or post and paling fences, erected and made around or about any garden, orchard, plantation or settlement, must be five feet high, well staked and ridered; or, otherwise, must be five feet high, and locked and braced at the corners, and from the ground to the height of three feet, the rails or logs must not be more than four inches apart, except in cases of paling, the holes must not be more than two inches asunder. If the fence is made with a ditch, the same must be four feet wide, and the fence five feet high from the bottom of the ditch, and three feet high from the top of the bank.

LOUISIANA. No legal fence is prescribed but every land owner has the right to compel contribution from adjoining owners for making and repairing walls and fences used in common. (*Revised Civil Code*, 1870, *Art.* 675-690.) If country estates are inclosed, common boundaries must be made at the expense of adjacent estates, but unenclosed estates are not bound to contribute thereto.

TEXAS. (*Rev. Stat.* 1879, p. 358.) *Article* 2431. Every gardener, farmer, or planter, shall make a sufficient fence about his cleared land in cultivation, at least FIVE FEET high, and make such fence sufficiently close to prevent hogs from passing through the same.

Concerning BARB WIRE FENCE, (*Rev. Stat.* 1879, *Appendix* p. 12) the following exists. *Section* 1. Three strands of Barbed Wire, with posts not further apart than fifteen feet, with a board not less than four inches wide, and one-half an inch thick, hung to the top wire; or two strands of Barbed Wire and a board not less than five inches wide and one inch thick; or two strands of Barbed Wire and a rail; when boards are used, three boards, to be not less than five inches wide and one inch thick, or four rails; if made of boards and rails, the posts to be not more than eight feet apart; when pickets are used, the pickets to be not more than six inches apart.

All fencing built within the provisions of this act, shall be not less than FOUR-AND-A-HALF FEET high, and shall be deemed a lawful fence—*and provided further*, that the interval between the posts in Barbed Wire fences, as provided in this section, may be increased or diminished by order of the Commissioners' Court of any county.

ARKANSAS. (*Digest* 1874, p. 598.) *Section* 3185. All fields and grounds kept for enclosures shall be inclosed with a fence sufficiently close, composed of sufficient posts and rails, posts and paling, palisades, or rails alone, laid up in the manner commonly called worm fence.

Sec. 3186. All fences composed of posts and rails, posts and palings, or palisades, shall be FIVE FEET high, and the posts shall be deeply and firmly set in the ground.

Sec. 3187. All fences of rails alone, commonly called worm fence, shall be FIVE feet high.

Sec. 3188. Any landlord who shall fail to make the fence or enclosures around his land which may be in cultivation, in conformity to the last preceding three sections, shall, upon conviction thereof, be fined in any sum not less than twenty, nor more than fifty dollars. (*Act Apr.* 25, 1873.)

MISSOURI. (*Statute* 1877, p. 197.) *Section* 1. Provides that all fields and inclosures shall be inclosed by hedge, or with a fence sufficiently close, composed of posts and rails, posts and palings, posts and planks, posts and wires, palisades, or rails alone, laid up in the manner commonly called a worm fence, or of turf with ditches on each side, or of stone or brick.

Sec. 2. All hedges shall be at least four feet high, and all fences composed of posts and rails, posts and palings, posts and wire, posts and planks, or palisades, shall be at least four feet and a half high.   *   *   *   Worm fence shall be at least five feet high to the top of the rider, or if not ridered, shall be five feet high to the top of the top rail or pole, and shall be locked with strong rails, poles, or stakes. Those composed of stone or brick, shall be at least four feet and a half high.

TENNESSEE. (*Amended code*, 1877.) *Section* 1682. Every planter shall make and keep a sufficient fence around his land in cultivation, and a sufficient fence shall be as follows: A common worm or crooked rail fence shall be FIVE FEET high; a post and plank, or post and rail fence, shall be FOUR FEET high; and such fences shall be of ordinarily sound and substantial material; a stone fence shall be a substantial wall, three and a half feet high: *Provided*, that all fences shall be close enough for two and a half feet from the bottom, to prevent hogs large enough to do damage, from passing through the fence.

KENTUCKY. (*General Statutes* 1873, p. 543.) *Section* 1. Every strong and sound fence of rails, or plank, or iron, five feet high, and being so close that cattle or other stock cannot creep through; or made of stone, or brick, four and one-half feet high, or a ditch three feet deep and three feet broad, with a hedge two feet high, or a rail, plank, stone or brick fence, two and a half feet high, on the margin thereof, the hedge or fence being so close that cattle cannot creep through, shall be deemed and held to be a lawful fence.

The Lumber Supply.

The amount of logs secured for the season of 1880-81 in the principal logging districts of the Northwest, is as follows:

District.	New Logs.	Old Logs.	Total.
Mississippi Valley	1,673,000,000	568,500,000	2,241,500,000
Lake Superior	147,500,000	5,000,000	152,500,000
Lake Michigan	1,664,000,000	287,500,000	1,951,500,000
Eastern Michigan	1,582,200,000	217,250,000	1,799,450,000
Wolf River.	115,000,000	20,000,000	135,000,000
Total	5,181,700,000	1,098,250,000	6,279,950,000

If we add to this the amount of summer logging, the total cannot fall much short of 7,450,-000,000 feet. According to the Census report, there are only 81,650,000,000 feet of standing pine in three States, Michigan, Wisconsin, and Minnesota; therefore the amount of logs cut annually becomes a matter that is both interesting and serious. At the present rate, admitting the correctness of all the figures, and making no allowance for continual growth, the lumber industry *can extend over only twelve years more.* It is a fact **well** known to all interested in the preservation of our forests, that new belts should be planted to pine, or else we shall shortly suffer greatly for one of the necessities of life.—*American Agriculturist, June,* 1881.

Early use of Wire Fence.

The Journal of the Franklin Institute (Philadelphia), Jan., 1830, referring to a patent for a wire fence, says: "There is no novelty in the invention. Fences of wire were common in England many years ago. They were also used in this country, particularly in the neighborhood of Philadelphia, fifteen or twenty years since. Messrs. White & Hazard, who at that time had a Wire Manufactory at the falls of the Schuylkill, erected many wire fences in the neighborhood of their establishment."

An Early Fence Law.

"Remembering the severall inconviencyes and multiplicity of suits and vexations arising from the insufficiency of fences, which to remedy in the old town hath been so difficult, yet in our removal to the place appointed for the new towne may easily be prevented It is therefore ordered that all fences, generall and particular, at the first setting up shall be mayde so sufficient as to keep out all manner of swyne and other cattle, great or small, and at whose fence or part of fence any swyne or other cattle shall breake through, the party owning the fence shall not only bear and suffer all the damages, but shall further pay for each rod so insufficient, the somme of two shillings. It is likewise ordered that the owners of all such cattle as the town shall declare unruly or excessively different from all other cattle shall pay all the damages that unruly cattle shall do in breaking through fences." (*Town Records of Newbury, Mass.*, 1644.)

The French Land System.

Theorists, advocating the open field system, so frequently draw their illustrations from the French land system, that a view of French rural life will be of interest. Says a late writer:

"The interest and economy of the French are wonderful, and their power of paying their war debt has attracted the admiration of our people, who have a much more serious debt on their hands. It is error, however, to ascribe the thrift of the French people to the subdivision of their land.

"It appears that of the 38,000,000 of people, 4,000,000 are able to live without work or business, and that 20,000,000 of the people live in the country, and are near'y all of them cultivators of land. It is well that before we are carried too far in admiration of French agriculture, and the minute divison of land, we find out how it is that the farmers there are liable to send away so much of the fruits of their three acres and a half ; how they send to England in a year $11,000,000 worth of butter and $9,000,000 worth of eggs. We shall find that it was by *going without themselves.* The ability of the French peasants to live on a cheap and limited fare is almost proverbial, and they are by necessity cut off from the means of acquiring knowledge, and are subjected by their incessant toil, and the character of it, to a degraded social life. It may be cheerful, for there is no knowledge of any better."

An English artist, who has resided many years in a rural district in France—Phillip Gilbert Hamerton—says of the peasant farmers tha' they farm profitably "only by incessant toil, and a wonderful sobriety, frugality, and self-denial." Even the middle classes live with great frugality, but their food is well prepared, "cookery with them is a well understood art, but the peasantry are utterly ignorant of it," "they being frugal above all things, avoid it, as an indulgence which is not for them." The poorest laborer's family in America is far better supplied than the French farmer's family, though the latter may own the soil.

ERRATA.